Through My Eyes:

tragedy to triumph

BY

ERIN ROXBOROUGH

Watersprings
PUBLISHING

Through My Eyes: Tragedy to Triumph

Published by Watersprings Publishing,
a division of Watersprings Media House, LLC.
P.O. Box 1284 Olive Branch, MS 38654
www.waterspringsmedia.com
Contact publisher for bulk orders and permission requests.

Editor credit: Dawn Adams

Photography credit: Tavon Ingram - Exquisite Imaging

Printed in the United States of America.

ISBN-13: 979-8-9859594-6-8

Table of Contents

Preface

What in the world would provoke me to open up the most intimate details of my life to a bunch of random people? Sure, I already know who you are. Most of you are "my Friends" from Facebook or Instagram. You may have purchased this book simply out of curiosity. You may be reading it because let's be honest, you find me intriguing… Don't lie. You can't quite put your finger on the why, but you're drawn to me. Or perhaps, it's out of boredom, and you have nothing to do during this pandemic. I get it.

Well, get a glass of wine, sit back, and kick your feet up. Just relax. I'm sure you've been vaccinated. Yep, I saw all of your vaccination cards posted just before I took my hiatus from social media. Whatever your reason for picking up this book, I want to thank you for the vote of confidence, and hopefully, I'll get you to the 2nd page.

Let me warn you, I'm prone to bouts of random jokes and sporadic vulgarity wrapped in Black vernacular. But please don't allow this Catholic school girl's potty mouth to distract you from the story of how I overcame seemingly insurmountable odds to claim victory.

Now, this is certainly not a how-to guide on how to overcome adversity. I can barely piece together how I got from point A to point B. How can I possibly tell someone else how to get there? As a matter of fact, I didn't have a plan at all. Looking back, it was like speeding down a hill on a mountain bike with no brakes and crashing into Z, but somehow, I survived. So, I'm here to share with ya'll how I worked my way back from Z to F, then to E and D to today, collecting a few bruises and bandages along the way. I'm good, though, or at least I think I'm good. Nah, I am well. Nowadays, I am constantly giggling. It's my quick reaction when I find myself in extremely emotional situations. I cannot control it. It almost appears as if I don't take anything seriously. That's a far cry from the awkward bespectacled nerd girl I used to be. *Damn girl, why you so serious all the time?* People were always asking me that question, but if they only knew how I longed to live the carefree lives that they did. My life was as dull and monotonous as the nursery rhymes on 45s that my mom collected. Most 45s had one, maybe two songs on each side. Well, these felt like a million rhymes on one side. One after the other, they droned on and on, then suddenly, I'd hear, "Turn the record over, begin on the other side. (Ding), You may turn the page." I can't help but laugh as I think about it now. Have you ever really listened to the words of a nursery rhyme? Some of them are horrendous! Just like some of the crap I've been through. I mean, Humpty Dumpty sat on a wall. Humpty Dumpty had a great fall, and nobody could put him back together again! Sorry, Humpty! I put my life back together. Now that I have all this joy in my life, shouldn't I share what I've been through with others? Of course, I should. It may do some good, or we can just laugh our asses off.

My identity has been shaped significantly by a few people and experiences that created a lasting impact. Some are positive, and some have been traumatic; either way, the footprints are left on my soul.

1

That's My Mama

"Erin, let's take the bags to the Salvation Army. Oh, Phooey," Mom *lamented.*

"What's wrong?" I inquired.

"I forgot to put a stamp on the envelope for my church dues.

That's my mom. A God-fearing, non-drinking, fancy-dress-wearing Christian. My example of honor and sacrifice. At 5 feet 7 inches, she stands taller than the average woman. Her supple cocoa complexion belies her 75 years on this earth. She can easily pass for someone in their mid-60s.

I was supposed to have been born on her birthday, but instead, I came into the world two days later, on May 25th. She says that I am her Glory-gift. She is my best friend and mall buddy. I cannot imagine my life without her.

January 16th, 1981. I don't recall ever being so cold. As I wiggled my little seven-year-old fingers bound in mittens and stuffed in my coat pockets, I thought this must be what they mean when they say child abuse. My mom had slathered so much Vaseline on my face, my eyelashes were clumped, and my lips stuck together whenever I tried to say something. I must have looked like a short shiny mummy waddling through the snow and frigid temperatures as we (my mom, her best friend, and me) made our way down Pennsylvania Ave alongside twenty-five thousand other people rallying to make the late Dr. Martin Luther King's birthday a national holiday. All I knew was that everyone said Dr. King was a "mighty" man, but I wondered if he was so mighty, why didn't he know I was sleepy and freezing? Why couldn't this wait till it was summertime? I was much too young to grasp this day's significance, but I knew it had to be important for my mom to have me out there in the peak of winter. I would come to understand more as I got older just why she and so many others walked and marched on that day. If I counted all the days and nights my mom and I had walked in the bitter cold, I knew this one had to be the most meaningful for her.

"Eeeaaaaarrriinnnn, it's 10am, the day is damn near over; get up, rise, and shine!" Mom commanded in the drawn-out lilting accent borrowed from our hilarious Caribbean neighbors. Whenever I heard that call, I knew my assignment; get out of the house and search for something productive to do. That was every summer of my teen years, weekend adventures on foot or by city bus to neighborhood bookstores and museums. Rain, sleet, or scorching sun, my mother did not tolerate idleness of any kind. As far back as I can remember, Sundays were for God and learning. Yes, I can still hear James Cleveland, 1979's *God is....* *My protection. God is my today and tomorrow. God, my God, is my all and all. God is the joy and the strength of my life. He removes all pain, misery, and strife. He promised to keep me, never to leave me and He'll never ever come short of His word.*

Like clockwork, I would be awakened by Mom's breakfast menu alarm, "Erin, come and get your plate of homemade biscuits, fried apples, scrambled eggs with cheese grits!" Sometimes she'd switch it up and serve pancakes.

By 10am, we would be in church, and by 12:15pm, we would be on the 16th Street bus headed downtown to the Museum of Natural History or to see the latest African American art exhibit. No matter how hard I wished I could just go home and sleep like the other kids who left Sunday school, it wasn't happening. Mom believed in taking advantage of every opportunity for education. One of her favorite maxims is, "The early bird catches the worm, Erin!" I remember it as if it were yesterday. While everyone else was at home watching football, I looked at dinosaur bones and studied thousand-year-old rocks.

Every single day at 6pm, a full-balanced meal was on the table. Mom rarely missed a day of cooking. You would have thought there were at least five people in our family, but it was just us. She believed in leftovers. Truth is, most times, the food tasted better the next day anyway. She provided me with everything I needed. She modeled strength for me, not that she didn't struggle or sacrifice because she did. But the difference from some single parents is that my mom did not dwell on past regrets, harbor resentment, or display any remnants of bitterness. Most wouldn't blame her if she had; however, she encouraged me from a place of resilience and nurtured and poured into my strengths. Her approach to parenting me led me to believe she didn't pay much attention to my weaknesses.

Mom's strategy to keep this latchkey kid out of the streets and out of trouble was to enroll me in as many academic enrichment programs as she could find. She was hellbent on developing my intellect because she wanted me to know I had a brain and how to use it. High Achievement Program, or HAP for short, helped shape my identity quite a bit. HAP was designed to promote better reading and writing skills for students. I attended from 1985-1987. Some of my favorite memories were at HAP. I discovered my love for books like S.E Hinton's *The Outsiders* and *The War on Villa Street* by Harry Mazer. I was one of the only kids who actually wanted to read those books. I was captivated by the characters and drawn into their lives. So curious to see how the characters would play out in their lives. It was never my plan to sequester myself in books and learning programs, but my mom made me do it. As I think back, I'm glad she did. It exposed me to worlds beyond my own and ignited my interest in so much more.

My mom would leave these little notes of encouragement, scriptures, and prayers for me all over the house. *Erin, God is your father. You are loved. You can do all things through your father, your Christ who strengthens you.* I believed every one of them. I am convinced that my mom's prayers are the reason for many of my blessings. Those notes helped me stay out of trouble. Mom also bought me quite a few Bibles. I guess all those Bibles accomplished what she had intended because reading them sparked a deeper love in a higher power.

I don't recall anything specific about all the Bibles that mom had given me, but I do remember the little blue Bible. It was one of the only things that my biological dad ever bought me. I held onto that little blue book for years. I kept thinking that one day it would somehow bring my dad and me closer together.

When mom moved to DC from Rochester, New York, she became interested in the Catholic religion. It was a no-brainer that I would be enrolled in a Catholic School, more specifically, St. Augustine Catholic School on 14th and V Street NW DC. I attended from 1st through 12th grade. My mom sacrificed so much to keep me close to God. Nothing made a more lasting impression on me than attending St. Augustine Catholic Elementary School, so much so that I became a member of the oldest Black Catholic church in the Washington DC area. My mom had the late shift when I was younger, and we would often have to walk home at 11:30pm at night just to turn around and wake up at 6am to do it all over again. Mrs. Dyson, one of my few favorite babysitters, used to make me the most delicious tuna fish sandwiches. I remember her washing my face with a cold washcloth just before my mom would pick me up at night. It was something about that simple routine that made me feel loved and cared for and kept me going.

Mom worked at Children's Hospital as a nurse. During her tenure there, she came in contact with a lot of young teen moms. She provided them consistent non-judgmental support. She loved those girls. She would share their stories with me, and I listened intently. But I led such a weird lonesome, and mostly mundane existence much of the time that I mean I couldn't even imagine what those girls went through. My heart went out to them. I definitely couldn't imagine myself in their situation, and my mom did everything she could to make sure I never was.

Mom's sex education and "Keep Erin Wholesome Plan" was unique and untraditional, to say the least. One day she came home with copied pictures of STDS. She called to me from the living room with an urgency that told me I'd better hurry. As I entered the living room, she commanded, "Erin, go grab the encyclopedia! Grab the letter "C" and look up the word, Chlamydia!

"What?" How do you spell it?" I asked, confused.

"Erin, you find out and tell me what it is. HURRY UP!" Why people tell you to look up a word and don't give you the spelling, is CRAZY! I must have been like 12 or 13. This woman had me memorizing the names of sexually transmitted diseases *and* telling her what the symptoms were. YUK!!!! I wasn't a fan of her approach, but it definitely didn't hurt. But she had nothing to worry about with me. The thought of sex was far from my mind.

Another time, I was a bit older; I came home from school, and as my feet crossed the threshold, I heard, "Erin, I hope that you know that I am

NOT ready to be a grandmother, and if you bring a child in here, you will not have a place to live. DO YOU UNDERSTAND ME?" In that last line, mom punctuated each word for emphasis. I was dumbfounded. *What the hell just happened?* As I stumbled the rest of the way into the apartment, I couldn't find any words to respond, but I was involved in a full-blown dialogue with myself in my head. *First of all, I would have to do the thing to get pregnant, and secondly, why was she coming at me like this?* Sometimes Mom didn't know how to leave her work *at* work. I guess that seeing those young girls she mentored and dealing with all that comes with being a teen mom got to her. It got to me, too, and the thought of letting my mom down was enough motivation to stay away from all of that as a teen.

Critics say that the Scared Straight program isn't really effective in deterring criminal activity for "At Risk" children; however, the very idea of a program like that worked pretty darn well on a kid like me. I was scared of almost every damn thing. Like I said, I was mostly afraid of making choices that would disappoint my mother. Now don't get me wrong, I was not an angel by a long shot. Most days, I spent hours riding my bike all over the city while Mom was at work just to make sure I stayed out of trouble. But then there were the days when I would hang out with a few friends on the block instead of doing chores. You see, I wasn't so much risk averse, but I did take calculated risks. My mom's schedule was so routine that our neighborhood could set their clocks by her movements. Every day at exactly 7:45pm, a little blue Nova with my mom in the driver seat cruised through the alley. If I was out and about the streets, my homegirl Meka and the other neighborhood kids would sound the alarm. "Erin! Your mom is coming! Hurry up! When that alarm sounded, I knew I only had five minutes to get my yellow ass up to that apartment and see about those dishes or else.

2

That Catholic School Girl

"Yes, Erin, there's the word of God and here is my belt" Now go do your homework!"

I grew up going to Catholic schools. We were taught what we should and should not do. My mom would always provide that balance with her belt in her hand.

When I was in the 3rd grade, I was a rebel and questioned everything. The sacrament of Penance was coming up. My teacher says, "Erin, you must be prepared to recite the Act of Contrition and confess your sins to the priest." I said, "Nope! I am not ...no way, Hosea" I am not confessing anything to just that weekend prior, I had gone to the corner store and almost wiped them out. I had bags of chips, 2 boxes of lemon heads, some Boston Baked beans, and 3 packs of Now and Laters. There was no way I was gonna confess to a priest and risk my mom finding out! I was just like that little girl in the movie Crooklyn when she packed all of that stuff into her shirt. I proclaimed with conviction, "God is the only one who can forgive my sins. I am not telling any MAN what I did." I got a week's detention for talking back to the teacher.

I did eventually take my sacrament, but I did like everybody else and just lied. I knew if I was gonna be a Catholic, I had to keep my little white lies together. My mom always called them little white lies. Yes, she had books on the shelves about Christianity. Sure, it's the religion of our oppressors, but right next to that book would be the history of Black Catholics in this country. It's almost like this love-hate relationship with Catholicism. I'm sure many other people have gone through this strained kind of existence. Anyway, the more I read, the more I started to develop a strong cultural pride and love that really shaped who I am. Being a Catholic also had a very dark side. I mean, what kind of God was gonna punish me and require that I make myself so damned uncomfortable just to please others? I mean, it made me stagnant at times. I used to be so critical of myself, and most of it was so unnecessary, really.

My eyeglasses were as thick as coke bottles, and my classmates would always say that I could see into the future. They were sorta right about that, actually. When I got suspended in the third grade…yes, I was suspended in elementary school! It was my only suspension during my Catholic school years. There was this girl named Tandy. Tandy was loud and boisterous, with a tendency to pick on the quiet kids at school. On this particular day, I was the target of her ire. A group of us was playing at recess. I don't even remember where things went wrong or what was, but it quickly got out of hand. We were yelling at each other, and before I knew it, there was a chorus of kids chanting, "Fight! Fight!" I didn't see it coming. Tandy swung. I heard my glasses snap as her hand connected with my face, and in response, I punched her dead in her chest. Before the next punch could be thrown, one of the teachers interjected into our impending brawl and hauled us both to the principal's office. I was petrified. Now you may be thinking it was going to the office that had me in fear's grip, but you would be wrong. It was the very idea of having to tell my mother that she was going to have to pay for a new pair of eyeglasses.

When I was eleven, there was a new girl in our class. She had all the fly gear and dressed really nice! She lived in a big house on 16th Street. I literally remember the day I asked my mom, "Can you please get me a pair of high-top Reebok sneakers?"

Mom got quiet, which was rare for her. A few moments later, my mom says, "I have a better idea!" That next week she brought home a pair of yellow, high-top Gussini shoes. She had no idea she was setting me up for the ultimate "jonin" experience at school.

It was Tag Day, which was a free day when we could be out of uniform. The one day that I had to escape from that uniform was the day I had to wear shoes those Gussini shoes. I hated them. As I walked through the hall, a very rude and silly 8th-grade boy yelled, "Are those supposed to be Reeboks?"

I was so embarrassed and humiliated. It was just one more thing that made me stand out. My mother wasn't interested in buying me the Reeboks, and she didn't give a damn if my new friend or anyone else had a brand-new pair.

Middle School/Junior High

I'll never forget that day I was working on a school assignment at the Martin Luther King library on 10th and G Street downtown. I must have been in the 7th or 8th grade. I was hanging out in the library, focused on gathering the books and other materials for my assignment. I approached the librarian standing behind the desk. "Excuse me, sir, can you please help me find a book entitled, *The River Nigger*? I oozed confidence as the words rolled off my tongue and rang in the librarian's ears. The look on that white man's face, his brows lifted high, his complexion transformed to a light pinkish hue, and the corners of his mouth twitched as if holding in a chuckle. He looked directly at me, his tone heavy with gentle correction. "Young lady, I believe you're looking for *The River Niger*. It's a principal river in Western Africa."

I felt my face grow warm. I felt like an idiot. After that day, I swore that I would do my damnedest not to ever mispronounce any word…like ever again. In fact, I believe that day the seed was planted, driving my need to learn more about my ancestors and my history. If cell phones had been a thing back then, I would've had a dictionary app on my phone, and I began collecting dictionaries. I had them all around the house, and I bought pocket ones to carry in my purse. The pocket dictionaries got the most use because I literally took them everywhere I went. They were my version of a literary American Express card—I didn't leave home without it!

I believe that Black Catholic guilt haunted me in moments like these. At the same time, it somewhat propelled me to read and study more. It's that memory of the strict Catholic nun with her glasses perched on the tip of her nose staring me down, ruler in her hand demanding that I turn my hand over for a quick pop whenever I misbehaved in class! My identity as a Black Catholic has definitely changed from my teenage years to my mid-30s.

In my 8th grade year at St. Augustine, I had a small part in the Christmas play. I'd rehearsed my few lines for over a month and knew them well. My speech teacher had dispensed all kinds of advice for dealing with nervousness and stage fright, "Stare at the basketball goal across from the stage, take deep breaths, and so on." I was ready…or I should have been.

Showtime! The auditorium was dark, and the atmosphere was melancholy. I stood center stage, hidden in the shadows. I could barely make out figures in the audience, but I knew it was a big crowd. The sudden clicking-thud sound somewhat startled me as the stage lights turned on and illuminated me. Every muscle in my body froze, and my heart pounded inside of my chest so hard I not only felt it but heard it. I stood there, mouth gaped open, peering through the lenses of my quirky, somewhat oversized glasses, and stared into the abyss. To this day, I don't know why but feelings of shame for looking like my father overwhelmed me at that moment. It was followed by deep sorrow because I knew he wouldn't be there. He was never there. As the awkwardness of the moment grew, a barrage of thoughts stomped through my mind—*you're stupid, inferior, worthless, you can't do anything right*! I was convinced that the audience could hear my thoughts, and they didn't disagree. Although only a few minutes ticked by, it felt like hours. I began to pray under my breath to my God that I could relax. At that moment when I thought I might regain control, Catholic school guilt kicked in—*God was punishing me for missing church the Sunday before. I deserved to go completely blank and look like a total fool in front of the whole school.*

Once I was old enough to critically analyze Catholicism and its impact on my self-image, I was already in college. I began reflecting on my spirituality and learned to stop beating myself up for everything. I figured that if I read more about the history and herstory of Black Catholics in this country, then I could embrace it a bit more. My mother had grown up in a Pentecostal Church of Christ, and she didn't talk much about why she became interested in Catholicism. My summation is that I think she didn't want to do all of that shouting, so she left for a more mundane, low-key "AHHHMEN!!!!!!!!!"

Recess was held in the street directly in front of the school, and there were orange combs blocking the traffic from the U Street entrance and the 14th street entrance. It was the best time of our day unless those nuns or our teachers gave us a time out on what they called "The Wall."

The black poles ran along the front of the school. I'm not sure why they even gave it that name. At any rate, it wasn't but ten, fifteen minutes later; here comes another childhood friend since 3rd grade, stomping into the office because, yes, now she is getting suspended for something I had no clue about till we walked to the bus stop together. We both had a tendency to act sassy as ever, and we both got sent home for one week. I remember us saying to each other that we would go outside and rides our bikes. We stayed on the bike trail at Rock Creek Park and rode bikes throughout the summer and school year. I knew how to get around pre-gentrified DC very well. Well, we were free of school and happy as ever to be out. This week of being out of school while my mother was at work at the hospital felt like one of those early summer breaks in college. I took for granted all of this free time to not have any major responsibilities.

"Ah yea, I'm gonna sit here laid back to this nice mellow beat, you know, and drop some smooth lyrics 'cause it was '88, time to set it straight, you know what I'm saying? And ain't no half stepping…Word, I'm ready." I'm kidding, I was no Big Daddy Kane, but I always thought I was cool, but in actuality, I was pretty corny. I talked incessantly, well, to my very few friends.

I remember being on three-way for hours talking with one of my friends. Right now, I get warm fuzzies from those memories. I mean it would have been a much lonelier childhood for me had these friends not been in my life. "Meka" as we affectionately called Tameka, was always pestering me and asking what I was writing in the black and white speckled composition books that I carried everywhere. I would sit on the doorstep outside of her apartment building, jotting in my notebook while I waited for her to come home. I knew her schedule by heart. There were days I'd stare out of our living room window, watching and waiting for Meka to walk through the church parking so I could hang out with her or anyone really. As soon as I spotted her, I would fly out of our apartment, gallop down the stairs, holding my breath for the 20 seconds it took to go through the hall past that nasty, stinky a**** trash room. I knew that what was on the other side of that door would promise me a great future where I could be free. Most of my evenings were spent outside with Meka until our parents signed us up for jobs. Yep, I had to go to work.

My first job was as a teacher's aide at the Raymond Elementary School off of Spring Road in Northwest DC. I was so excited to finally be able to earn my own money for the first time!! It was the summer of 1988, I was 14 years old, and like so many DC teens, I was among tens of thousands of youth who had gotten summer jobs through the Marion Barry Summer Youth Employment. The program was designed to keep me and other "At Risk" DC youth off the street. I just knew that this was my ticket to buying anything I wanted and not having to ask my mom for it. I worked in the program every summer until I left for college in 1992.

Our duties were mainly clerical work and typing or something else I can't really remember. Luckily, we always had something productive to do with our time, and we thank God for it. My mother wasn't just about education. She was serious about me putting my pennies away. She insisted that I save at least half the money I earned that summer. She could care less how I spent the rest of the money. I knew, above all else, that she wasn't playing about me saving. When I cashed my first check, I hopped on my bike and raced to the Madness Connection on Georgia Avenue to get a Gilligan Island hat, like the ones the really cool and popular kids wore. I wasn't cool or popular… not the least bit, but I got my hat! I had my nickname, Roxy, written across the front. My second purchase was a pair of MC Hammer balloon pants and a few bright colored Michael Jackson Leave Me Alone shirts to match. Like I told you, I was a skinny little thing with bright red glasses and braces and totally one of the most awkward-looking girls in my class.

I did have a serious crush on this dude named Travis; our birthdays were two days apart. Almost every day, he would exclaim, "E, you gonna be my girl, right?"

"Okay, whatever you say, Travis," was my patent reply. Although we never really made it official, we would go to the Madness Connection and even buy matching green Guess jeans to wear. We thought we were the bomb.

Most of the dudes saw me like the little sister that they never had, though. I was a smart girl—the intelligent one; everyone told me so, and I believed it. This was the one thing that kept me focused on getting my education. That and the fact that my mother didn't give me any other option. It was either stay in school and do well, or give up my habit of living and breathing.

I wanted to be the happy-go-lucky teenager who had a mother and father who loved one another. I wanted to live in a beautiful house with a white picket fence, a two-car garage, and a cat. Yes, there always has to be a cat somewhere around. Meanwhile, in the real world, I buried my fear and insecurities under layers of lies and lies. I escaped into the characters of my books to get a sense of family. Some books I read made me appreciate my single-parent home. I tended to relate more to characters with close connections to one parent.

When I read *Manchild in the Promised Land* by Claude Brown, I connected deeply with the main character Sonny. Sonny grew up in the mean streets of Harlem; I was growing up in the not-always-so-friendly streets of Washington, DC. That book gave me so much hope because its main character resembled people I knew and showed me that even if you grow up in the hood, you can actually become some damn body and be successful.

3

Jean

I can hear it now, Beres Hammond's gritty tenor singing, "*I'd like to tell you a story about what one dance can do; one dance can do, after one dance on the floor, she came back wanting for more and more…*" and Jean beckoning me in her thick rhythmic West Indian accent. "Eearin! Come on, let's get it!" Jean loved Beres Hammond, the Jamaican reggae artist, so I loved him too. Jean was my babysitter from the time I was 9 until 10. Jean was my favorite of all the babysitters that took care of me as a child. She had this sweet and nurturing motherly disposition, and even though she didn't have children of her own, she made me feel safe and loved when I was in her presence.

Each day after school, my mom would drop me off at Jean's house, where I would stay while she worked the evening shift at the hospital. Jean would greet us at the front door and scoop me up in her arms with a big hug, then proceed to tell me what activities were on our agenda for the evening. Most nights, I sat at her dining table and did my homework while Jean cooked dinner. The aromas of the Caribbean recipes she made would waft throughout the house, making it hard for me to focus. I can't tell you how often I hurried to finish my homework so that I could devour her curry chicken and coco bread. The vibrant pink kitchen was Jean's happy place. Oh, how we would dance and sing and laugh in that tiny kitchen. I loved being with her. After our nightly "party," she would snuggle with me on the couch until I dozed off. She would hold me in her arms until my mom came around 11:30pm. I never said a word, but every time I hugged her neck tightly, it was my promise to keep her secret. As I think back, it was as if every time we danced, she forgot her troubles, and nothing else mattered.

Originally from Trinidad and Tobago, Jean and her husband lived in a house about a 10-minute walk from our apartment. They didn't have any children; maybe that's why she loved caring for other people's children so much. Jean was tall and fair-skinned. Her husband was tall as well but very dark. They were opposites; while Jean was lively and energetic, X was a somber and brooding giant. When he walked into a room, it was as if all the air got sucked out of the space. I can't recall him ever saying one word to me when I was in their home. I never spoke to him—I was too scared, not "hi" or "bye or please pass me the curry chicken." He scared me, plain and simple.

Every once in a while, I get nostalgic and pull out old photo albums. Whenever I come across a picture of my eighth or ninth birthday party, I can't remember which; my heart is strained between joy and dread. The picture is of all the kids standing around the table, eyeballing my huge vanilla birthday cake.

That year, my mom and Jean planned my birthday party together. It was in the basement of Jean's house on 14th and Spring Road, NW. On that day in May, her basement was lit up like never before. I remember being so excited seeing all the party decorations, balloons, and streamers everywhere! The atmosphere was electric. Everyone was laughing and talking and having so much fun. I don't ever recall Jean's basement filled with exuberant joy, laughter, or celebration like it was that day. That room was overflowing with love, and I felt it. I knew I was loved and cared for.

It's funny; my mom and I have an ongoing debate about the party. I don't remember any of my friends being at the party. The way I remember it is that all the children in attendance were invited by Jean. They were kids that she knew or maybe had cared for at some time or another. The rest of the people were friends of my mom's. I sure as hell don't remember who any of those people were. Of course, my mom says, "Oh, Erin, you don't remember such and such?" My response, " Uhhh, no, Mom." I'm just glad that whoever they are, they weren't eating all of my cake in that picture."

I remember that day well because it was one of the only days without a dark shadow filling the basement air. There were so many evenings that began light and fun but inevitably turned that house into a preview of a prize-fighting match. It would begin with Jean's husband picking at her and taunting her about some small thing or other and then the blowup would come. I would often stand at the top corner of the stairs, watching and trembling, as I listened to the low rumblings of the argument brewing, wishing it would all just stop! As the arguments continued, I would hear agonizing whimpers breaking through his thunderous shouts.

One evening, after I had settled in for my usual nap, I was startled from my drowsy slumber by a different sound. One I'd never heard before. I didn't know what it was then, but now I know it as the sound of terror. I jumped up from the sofa where I had been resting and ran to the stairs. I slowly made my way to the bottom step, tipping as quietly as I could. As my small sock-covered feet touched the last step, I froze. There was my beloved Jean, stretched out as if she were making snow angels on the bed. Her hands and feet were tied to the bed posts with string or something, and she was partially clothed. Her skirt had been pushed up around her waist, and she was exposed. Her husband struck her repeatedly about the head and face with his hand as he forced himself on her. My heart pounded so hard I thought it would pop out of my chest as I stood there, unable to move. I felt helpless as I squeezed my eyes tight, trying to purge the sight from my mind. X continued the relentless assault on his wife, seemingly oblivious to the fact that a child was present and that his heinous act changed her forever. The innocent child that I was disappeared into herself. From that day forward, I began locking away bits and pieces of myself and bottling up my feelings. It was the only thing I could do to keep the horror of that night from destroying me.

My time with Jean was bittersweet. I did my best to keep her secret, but the weight of that burden was enormous. I couldn't tell my mother what had happened because I just knew that she would take my Jean away from me. It had been difficult for my mom to leave me in the care of someone else from the beginning. But she worked long hours and that was her only option as a single parent. She took care to choose babysitters that were kind and caring and whom she could trust. She had no way of knowing what was going on under Jean's roof, and I was certainly not going to tell her. I felt that everything I witnessed was so very wrong, but I couldn't bring myself to tell anyone. Maybe I was confused or scared; the truth is I was both. At the tender age of 9, I thought it was up to me to protect Jean by keeping the secret. After the incident, I was no longer scared of X; I was absolutely terrified of him. I would have conversations where I would tell myself to obey him if he were to ever utter a word in my direction so as not to get Jean in trouble. I made sure that I always obeyed Jean to eliminate any possibility of causing him to pay attention to me. Whenever he was around, I would try to make myself invisible by blending into the furniture and avoiding eye contact at all costs. After a while, he wasn't around as much. I don't know if it was Jean who kept him away from me or that he avoided me, himself because he knew that I knew the secret and he didn't want to risk other people knowing what I knew.

One afternoon, Jean and I were alone in the house. After I had finished my homework, I went searching for her. I found her in the bedroom, seated at the vanity, putting on makeup. I watched her for a few minutes, layering on foundation on her beautiful face.

"Can I have some?" I asked innocently. She smiled and said,

"You are beautiful just the way you are, Erin!" She said softly. "When you get older, you're going to look sooooo pretty in your makeup!" She assured me with a loving smile.

When I get older? I thought I know that would be a no." I continued to watch her put on layer after layer attempting to cover up the bruises left by the man who was supposed to love and care for her. But no matter how much she put on, I could still see the evidence of the hell she was living. I wanted to forget at that moment that she had to do that often. When I think about it, maybe she didn't want my mom to see her bruises, either, or anyone for that matter. I remember there were days when she kept the house so dark you could barely see anything. There were other times when she would cover her face. I guess that she thought that it would be impossible for anyone to notice her bruises, and maybe it worked because no one ever said anything.

My mom would pick me up every evening around 11:30pm, and we would walk or take the bus back to our apartment. We usually traveled home in silence, which was just fine for me; if we didn't talk, I wouldn't be forced to lie. Lying to my mom was not really on my agenda. One night sometime much later, the secret became too much for my little nine-year-old self to carry. I poured out the story of what I'd witnessed to my mom. I never went back, and I never saw Jean again.

Unfortunately, I was haunted by the events of that day well into my teenage years. I believe that's when I begin to develop so many screwed-up beliefs about love and relationships. I was exposed to sexual violence before I really even knew what sex was, and I now know that I learned, indirectly, from Jean's husband that sex is not a loving act shared between a man and a woman but a weapon to control and to hurt.

Over the years, I've rarely discussed this experience because I never wanted anything to reflect badly on my mom in any way. You know how people always ask, "Where was the mother?" Well, she was right there protecting me. She didn't get angry or upset with me; she simply never took me back to Jean's. One night, in 7ᵗʰ grade, while trying to avoid helping in the kitchen, my mom began calling for me. "Erin, come get your plate! My sassy 13-year-old self tried to act as if I hadn't heard her summons, but she persisted. "Erin! I have some bad news to share with you. It's, it's about Jean." The words slowly trailed off her tongue and pierced my heart.

Suddenly, I was overwhelmed by memories of my younger days snuggling up with Jean and the two of us dancing and singing to Beres Hammond.

"Erin, she is no longer with us."

"She's dead?" I inquired my mind heavy with disbelief and confusion. My heart was broken. Mom went on to explain that she'd found out from a friend. Jean had been murdered by her husband. I lamented Jean's life and what I had witnessed. I pondered how she had become a victim of domestic violence. I still remember that sunken feeling in the pit my stomach. I wanted to die. Jean loved me, and I believed that revealing her secret would only hurt her more. But somewhere deep in me, I blamed myself. *What would have happened if I had told my mom earlier? Why didn't anyone in her family help her or tell her that it was okay to divorce him? Why didn't she leave?* I agonized over the what-ifs for years. Jean was dead. Dead, just like the love that I yearned for from my father. A broken spirit will be exposed to anything.

Jean was precious to me. Unfortunately, there are so many more Jeans out here. We all know Jean; she is our sister, our best friend, our co-worker, and our neighbor.

When I was in college, I wrote this piece just for her, and I remember presenting it as part of a lecture on campus about domestic violence.

For Jean

*He shoved pennies down her throat as his groping hands tied her to the
bedpost immediately after stainless steel beatings turned her Black and Blue*

All I heard from her was a little whimper, pleading for me not to tell.

He dragged her down merciless flights of stairs like old luggage;

her feet made no move to go anywhere

All I heard from her was a whimper pleading for me not to tell.

I saw expensive diamonds in her eyes

I could not tell a soul how expensive she really was

she always told me that she could not afford diamonds

all I heard from her was a little whimper pleading for me not to tell.

I shoved pennies down my own throat

As I swallowed her Black and Blue

Cause we couldn't afford to tell anyone

*Wikipedia defines domestic violence, also referred to as domestic abuse or
family violence or other abuse in a domestic setting, such as a marriage or
cohabitation, a coercive form of marital rape.*

It is important to raise awareness of violence against women. Violence
or abuse in any form has serious health consequences for the victim. It is
also so important to know the different types of violence. Violence of any
sort is unacceptable.

4

Other People's Children

Ask anyone in the neighborhood where I grew up, and they would tell you that, more often than not, I would have four or five kids strapped to my hip. I definitely was a different kind of teenager.

There were two other families in our apartment building who had children. I was older than all of them and I felt an obligation to take care of the younger kids because I knew what it was like not having a dad around. There were five kids in all in my grassroots babysitting service. One of the families lived on the first floor, and there were three kids, Paul (13), Aisha (12), and Pierre (10). Their parents were divorced, and they were being raised by their single mother, who was originally from Guyana. The other family was a two-parent household, and they had come from the Caribbean as well. If I recall correctly, their dad was from Jamaica, and their mom was from Trinidad. They had two kids, Mikey (10) and Kimberly (8). Kim had a learning disability, but it didn't stop her from rolling with the rest of the crew. On any given Saturday, you could find me riding the S2 (16th Street) bus with my kids in tow, headed to a museum on the Washington Mall. Now at that time, a one-way bus ride to the Washington Mall was sixty cents. I always had bus fare for myself but not for the kids I collected, so I would pretend like I couldn't find my money, and then I'd proclaim to the kids, "Aww, we will have to get off the bus!" On cue, Pierre would start whimpering, and in seconds, he'd be wailing. Frustrated but compassionate, the bus driver would just give up and let us all ride for free.

We did it so many times that the bus drivers on the route got hip to us and just let us ride for free from that point on. One rare Saturday afternoon, I decided to forego the regular museum trip to get some studying in. Just as I was getting into my little study groove, I was interrupted by loud banging on the door accompanied by high-pitched calls, "Erin! Erin!" I ran to the door as fast as I could. When I opened the door, Paul, Aisha, Kim, and Mikey started screaming frantically, "Quick, hurry, come help Pierre! They hurt him real bad!" I galloped down the dark stairway from our 3rd-floor apartment and sprinted down the street, following the kids to the corner store. My heart and head were pounding as all kinds of horrible thoughts of what could have happened crisscrossed my mind. As I rounded the corner and I started yelling, "What happened to my little brother?" Who did this to him? Not a soul said anything and I was totally in bewilderment about how I myself felt like such a coward in school and rarely stood up for myself, but when there's a kid involved, I'm the Incredible Hulk. There was blood, albeit very little, on the side of his head. He had been crying his eyes out after being called a crybaby and bullied by some bigger kids. Pierre was actually a crybaby. He was the middle child in his family. He had huge brown innocent eyes and a look of concern on his face all the time. His huge head was so adorable. I always told him his brains were extraordinary, and that's why kids teased him about his head. I loved him like the little brother I had always wanted.

I hugged him, walked him upstairs to our apartment, and ran into my mom's room to grab the first aid kit. I cleaned his small wound and even applied a bandage.

"I love you sis," Pierre whispered in staccato, trying to stop crying.

"I love you too, Pierre, always." Pierre ended up just fine. In fact, he grew up to be quite a scholar. I can still remember receiving a beautiful letter from him during his freshman year at Morehouse College. It started -

"Dear big sis" you are the reason I'm here." Pierre would later help me draft my very first syllabus for a class.

Even though I was the oldest kid in my building, I didn't make a conscious decision to become the big sister to all the younger ones. It happened organically. We came together and formed our own little family of sorts. Saturdays with my little surrogate siblings helped me escape the reality of being an only child without a father's presence in my life. Those children, unbeknown to them, became my motivation to want so much more out of life, to dream and to believe in love.

Every spring, toward the end of school, I knew it was time to find a summer job. Just like clockwork, my mom would storm into my bedroom; it was usually a Saturday morning. "Get up, rise & shine!" she would chant. "Early bird gets the worm; your summer job is waiting for you!"

This particular spring Saturday morning, I remember grabbing the Yellow Pages after I got up. For those of you under 40, the Yellow Pages were huge bulky books that listed all the phone numbers of businesses in the area. They were sectioned by the type of business. You would page through it to find what you were looking for. They were so big sometimes I would use them as breakfast or dinner trays. That day I flipped the page's right to the childcare section. I ran my fingers down each page line one by one and dialed every daycare center listed. I meant business, so I let that phone ring till someone answered. That's how I found Virginia Walden Ford, Ms. Ginny, as she was affectionately called. When Ms. Ginny answered, I blurted out with more confidence than I knew I possessed, "I'm Erin, I'm 17, and I attend Archbishop Carroll Highschool. I'm an A student. I'm looking for a summer job. I'm reliable, friendly, and ready to learn. I've been working with children since I was 14 years old, I worked at Marie Reed Childcare Center in NW DC and Raymond Elementary School off of a Spring Road." It felt like I was doing a pitch for a commercial or, better yet, that I was in a commercial. That one from the 80s where the guy is talking so fast you could barely make out a word here and there. I was talking so fast Ms. Ginny could not get a word in. Just when I inhaled to fill my lungs for part two of my spiel, Ms. Ginny edged her way into the conversation.

"Erin, you sound like just the person with the energy that we need." Ms. Ginny chuckled. Well, I didn't have to do any more convincing because Ms. Ginny hired me right away. After a couple of weeks, she trusted me enough to give me the key to the center so that I could open the early for her. Of course, this was long before parents dropped their children off at 6am, but I believe she did it to build my confidence. It made me feel good about myself. Yep, the awkward bespectacled, lanky-long-legged teenager, who always had a bunch of kids following behind like the pied piper, was large and in charge! I found a childcare center where their focus was to hire young people from the community for training.

Ms. Ginny had a twin sister, Ms. Harrietta Lindsey. These amazing twin sisters opened Wee Luv Daycare in September 1991 with a dream and a vision. Their mission was to launch a Black female-owned business that served their own community and worked with children. A key piece of their vision was to bring quality childcare to young families at reasonable rates. They were incredible to work with. In fact, Ms. Ginny would later become a prominent and influential education activist, advocate, and author.

In November 2017, when I heard that her life story was being made into a film, I wasn't surprised. The movie chronicled her real story as a struggling single mother from a low-income neighborhood, fighting for quality educational access for underprivileged students here in DC. Miss Virginia is, in fact, the heart and soul of the D.C. Opportunity Scholarship program. *Miss Virginia* was released in 2019; it was directed by R.J Daniel Hanna and starred Uzo Aduba in the role of Ms. Ginny. As I think about the role my mom played in my education, I realize there are striking resemblances between her and Ms. Ginny. Like, Ms. Ginny, my mom was bound and determined to ensure I got a quality education, and to do that, she sacrificed so much to keep me enrolled in private Catholic schools from kindergarten through high school.

As I look back now, I realize that parents fighting to get their children a good education was a common theme throughout my life and that of my closest friends. After I started working at, Wee Luv Daycare, my mom's loud 7am wake-up calls became a thing of my past because I started waking up before dawn on my own. Geesh! I don't know whether it was her repeated calls morning after morning that programmed me or the fact that I was excited to get up and go to work every day. Working with Ms. Ginny and Ms. Harrietta was one of the best summer jobs ever. I mean, I learned how to develop strong working relationships based on respect and admiration for others. I worked hard to be dependable and responsible because I wanted Ms. Ginny to be proud of me. It's a wonder sometimes how God works in our lives. Witnessing this Black woman empower herself and others in her community made an everlasting impression on me. I was empowered by simply being in her presence every day; I didn't really realize it then, but it was through her that I got a glimpse into my future profession.

That summer, my mom bought her first house in the same Brookland neighborhood in Northeast DC as Wee Luv Daycare. Our house was a short walk around the corner and an even shorter drive to my job. I don't believe I missed one day working there. On my first day on the job with Ms. Ginny, I made special note of the name; Wee Luv Daycare. As I walked into the building, I knew that I belonged there because that's exactly what I had been doing in the neighborhood all along. My passion for caring for Black children blossomed that summer, and from that time, it has only grown. It was around that time that I heard the term "At-Risk" kids. As I learned more and more about it, I recognized that I was an "at risk" youth myself. I began speaking up to and calling out anyone who didn't display a deep love for children. I became an advocate for black and brown children. By the time I turned 18, I had worked at five childcare centers in our neighborhood. Yep, I was the young woman who "took care of everybody's children."

I continued to advocate for children after I started my career. I would frequently slip a copy of Lisa Delpit's "Other People's Children" into a fancy bag with a candle and gift it to some of my colleagues. I'm still taking care of other people's children to this very day, and I will always remember the women who carved the way.

5

Grandmother

Once you know poverty, how can you ever really forget it? The smell of rotten milk and a pissy hallway brings you back to it. No, we were not impoverished, but we sure did struggle.

Grandmother, with her long curly brown hair and light complexion, was considered to be the epitome of beauty in her time. In fact, she was featured on the cover of the March 4th, 1954, issue of Jet magazine. The cover feature title was, *Do Lawyers Have the Prettiest Wives?* Yep, Mrs. June Roxborough, Detroit attorney's wife, was deemed one of the city's most beautiful women. You see, Grandmother had married an attorney, my grandfather, who eventually became a judge in the DC area. Grandmother lived a much different life, a much richer life in a myriad of ways. We were very different. When I was about 9 years old, court-ordered visitation was established with my biological dad. Shortly after, he took me to meet his mother for the very first time. I was so excited to meet her! I remember my mom prepping me for the visit and every visit after. "Now, Erin, remember to smile, be polite and keep your manners at all times."

My father and I rode in silence. I filled the time gazing out of the car window, watching Uptown DC disappear from my view and the "Gold Coast" appear in all its glory. The neighborhood known as the "Gold Coast" was a haven for affluent African Americans. The pristine lawns and sparkling windows of homes owned by doctors, lawyers, and other professionals lined the streets, reminding me of a picture I'd seen in a Better Homes and Gardens magazine once.

The house on Underwood Street was a lifetime away from our apartment in NW, DC. As my father pulled the car in front of the house, I felt as if I was going to jump out of my skin! I was so excited. I couldn't wait to start baking cookies and learning her secret recipes for her favorite dishes. We were going to be the very best of friends. She would take me on shopping trips and introduce me to her high society lady friends and acquaintances at the many luncheons she undoubtedly attended. I imagined telling my friends about the wonderful adventures that my grandma and I were going to have. They had all shared their grandma's stories; now I would have mine! On that short walk to the front door, I rehearsed and greeted her with enthusiasm and all the properness I could muster. I wanted her to be proud of me.

We entered and made our way through the house; I was in awe. There was a light sweet aroma that wafted through the rooms. The house was beautifully furnished but had a stiffness that warned me I would probably never stretch out on the couch. I timidly followed behind my father until she appeared seemingly out of nowhere. She was regal and just as pretty as I had imagined her to be. Trying to contain the excitement and love that welled up in me, I felt a Cheshire cat smile tug at the corners of my mouth and blurted out. "Hi, Grandma!"

She tilted her head downward, and with precise icy diction, she replied, "Grandmother. You are to call me, Grandmother. Do…you…understand?"

Each word dropped from her lips with finality, and any hope of being scooped up into her bosom to make up for all lost time plunged to the depths of my nine-year-old soul. At that moment, I was aware of an uneasiness, that would become a familiar and ever-present pain in the years to come.

For the life of me, I couldn't figure out what I had done and why she wouldn't allow me to call her grandma. Grandmother was so formal...too formal for me. My friends had affectionate names for their grandparents, like Nanna and Granny. But I had only Grandmother, and it made me feel that her love and approval would come with conditions.

I had yet to recognize this uneasiness, as feelings of less than-ness, unworthiness, and abandonment. But this precedent unbeknownst to me, had already been established with my father's absence in my life to date. I just did not belong there. I was not really one of them.

From that day forward, I knew I was simply a court-ordered obligation in their lives. The rebel in me screamed, *Hell! Just take me back to the pissy hallway! I'd rather be there than here!* But not even a squeak passed from my lips. That first meeting set the tone of our relationship somewhere between contentious and walking on eggshells at best.

The fact that I would never be comfortable at Grandmother's was solidified on my second visit. I was being my normal kid-self listening to some tunes on my bright yellow Sony Walkman as I came in and greeted Grandmother politely. Grandmother's response, "Why are you coming in here with that 'nigger box'?" I was shocked and confused, but of course, I kept quiet. There was absolutely nothing I could have said that would have made the situation better.

Over the next several years, I made what might be considered regular but not-so-frequent visits to my Grandmothers. I could only take her in small doses. On one such visit, Grandmother announced that she had errands to run, and I, of course, would accompany her. It was one of the few times that I rode with her, and it was my first experience with road rage. As we zoomed in and out of the heavy traffic on 16th Street heading towards Silver Spring, Maryland, a 20-minute reel of curse words flowed from her mouth about how she needed to reach her destination. I swear, at one point, she had to be going 60mph flying past the other cars. Then I heard sirens blaring behind us and getting closer. "Grandmother! What are you doing?" I yelled as a fire truck, and an ambulance whizzed by. Grandmother didn't miss a beat; she hit the gas and swooped in directly behind the ambulance. The ambulance driver maneuvered the emergency vehicle through the traffic by driving on the yellow road lines, and without any hesitation, so did Grandmother. I gripped the door handle for dear life, petrified that we would either crash or go to jail! Let me say this, I have never been arrested, and if it were to ever happen, I'll be damned if it is because of someone else's negligence.

Despite her beautiful exterior, Grandmother was an incredibly troubled soul. When I was 10, she drove me to the St. Jude Monastery because, according to her, she needed to sit me down to have a talk. Most of what she said, I will not share here simply out of respect for my mother; if you've paid attention so far, you can guess that she did not speak well of my mother. You know, some grown folks have no idea of how their words play on children. She called herself explaining my parents' relationship. Why she felt it was her place to do so, I'll never know. It was a conversation that definitely should not have occurred for my prepubescent mind, body, and soul. It was hard enough dealing with the reality of not having my father, her son, as a loving, actively engaged parent in my life while my mom worked and struggled to provide for us. This little talk equated to mental and emotional abuse and would only be the beginning of an uphill struggle with depression for me. Most decent people don't really need to take a child development course to understand how emotional scars can affect a child's self-esteem. I will say this, I was smart enough to never allow anyone to slander my mother, that's for damn sure. I wasn't exactly the sassy, talk-back type, at least not to adults; however, in my head, I maintained clear differences between the moral and immoral.

Grandmother banked at Industrial Bank. At one time, it was the largest black-owned bank in the country. I remember learning about Industrial Bank in one of my classes at St. Augustine. By the time I reached high school, I had a deep passion for my African American history and a strong cultural pride instilled from my mom reading books like *The Life of Nat Turner* and *Nzinga of Angola*. She had always stressed to me that Black is beautiful in all shades, shapes, and sizes. Grandmother nor my biological father ever uttered a single word to me about embracing my heritage, my melanin, or how to show the world exactly what Black Excellence looks like. It's quite ironic when I think about it because, on paper, the Roxboroughs was the epitome of Black Excellence.

I took every opportunity to share the cultural nuggets I learned with anyone who was within earshot. That is anyone except Grandmother. Whenever I'd try to share even the smallest piece of black history or show pride in the culture, she would cut me off in mid-sentence. Grandmother wasn't interested in our history or in me, for that matter. It happened so frequently that I took notice and stopped trying. When we were together, I'd stare out the window, daydream or pretend to be somewhere else, all while maintaining my manners, smiling, and being ever so polite. Still had a hunger to know who she really was.

One Saturday, while at the library, I had this brilliant thought! *If I could get into Grandmother's head and understand her, then just maybe I could understand her son.* I asked the librarian for *The Black Bourgeoise* by E. Franklin Frazier. I was driven to learn about folks who were so different than any of the people I had ever encountered in my life. I was used to being around down-to-earth, everyday hardworking poor folks. Often when I would read this type of stuff, my teachers would commend me on my sophisticated choice of literature. I have to admit I was flattered, but little did they know that I was just trying to understand my crazy family better.

As I have also told you, I didn't really share much about the things that bothered me with my mom, especially things associated with Grandmother. I didn't want my mother to have to deal with anything more than what was on her plate. As you can imagine, my relationship with Grandmother became more strained as I got older. If I complied with her wishes and agreed with her point of view, she would demonstrate her approval by pulling out her checkbook. I recall on a number of occasions, she gave me $1000.00 checks after I had evidently done something that warranted her stamp of approval. I'd take the checks home, and my mother would have me deposit them directly into my savings. But the very minute that I had an opposing thought, challenged Grandmother to think differently, or barely hinted that she might not be correct, I was summarily taken out of the will. One month I was in; the next, I was out. We went round and round on the June Roxborough you're-out-of-my-will-ride for close to eight years. Her constant criticism and emotional torture intensified through my teenage years and became almost unbearable. I was never fully at ease with my grandmother; she seemed to have disdain toward me. In hindsight, maybe that's because she wasn't really ever comfortable in my presence either. If I'm honest, I *was* a tad bit envious of my friend Tameka. I mean, she would speak so lovingly about her Nanna while I would sit there wondering what in the hell had I done to deserve *Grandmother*. I mean, I never harbored any jealousy or hatred towards anyone, really, but damn.

However, whatever her issue was with me, at least once a year, Grandmother would invite me to help with the annual Easter Roll at Howard University or some other community event. You see, Grandmother was a member of The Doll League. The League's mission was to support young women and children in need, and each year they sponsored the Easter event along with the D.C. Department of Recreation. The event was attended by more than 1000 kids from all over the city every year. There would be free food, fun rides, face painting, and Disney characters roaming the grounds making sure the kids had fun. The best part for me was that I was one of the volunteers who donned a Disney costume. I would always recruit my Drama Club friends like Chris Buchanan, Stephanie Braham, and Chris Grayton from Archbishop Carroll High School to help as well. We would meet at Grandmother's house a day or so before the roll to try on the costumes and choose our character for the event. I chose to play Goofy every year. I would drive Tin Lizzie while my friends and other volunteers dressed as Donald Duck, Mickey Mouse, and other characters created quite a spectacle as we raced our miniature cars. The children encouraged us, yelling and cheering for their favorite character to win. We had such great times hanging together, bringing the characters to life for the kids. It was also one of the few times that Grandmother's and my view of the world were in sync, if only for a few hours or so.

Chris Buchanan was the only friend that knew just how tumultuous my relationship with my grandmother was. He was the listening ear and strong shoulder I leaned on when I needed to scream, cry and vent. Chris' sarcastic sense of humor and deep resounding laugh kept me in stitches and helped take my mind off my troubles. Whenever the others would go on and on about how incredible it must be for me to be a Roxborough, he would give me a knowing look or grin. Sure, we're out playing these Disney characters bringing joy to children on Easter and then the next minute, I might get cursed out uhm, because of my hairstyle, my clothes, or any other random thing. Despite her prim and proper exterior, Grandmother was well-versed in the artistry of profanity, and the volatility of her mood swings left me feeling exhausted. Chris knew my secret and the silent weight I carried, just wanting to be loved and accepted by my father and grandmother.

Most, if not all, of the holiday dinners I attended at Grandmother's house, were characterized by conversation centered on the Roxboroughs' work and their other affairs. I, Erin Roxborough, was a guest at the table. I spoke when I was spoken to, and I kept my manners, just as my mother had instructed. I was rarely spoken to, and even more rare was the occasion when I was asked anything about my life or my dreams. In fact, I don't recall ever having an actual meal with Grandmother. I did offer to cook with her on a number of occasions or do anything with her in hopes of forging a loving relationship. That definitely never actualized. I was always disappointed that my attempts to truly connect with her failed time after time.

I remember one particular Thanksgiving during my teenage years. As usual, my mom gave me bus tokens and sent me to Grandmother's with a homemade cake as a token of her love. That year it was a vanilla frosted cake. I had become slightly irritated with my mom's insistence on continuing to show kindness to this woman because I didn't think that Grandmother was deserving. Hmph, I can hear my mom right now, "Erin, that's not the point." Anyhow, most times, I was just irritated that I had to carry that damn cake across the city on the bus.

When I arrived at the house, I greeted the family politely and delivered the "kindness cake" to Grandmother. Shortly after, we sat down at the table for dinner. The usual hum of Roxborough conversations was in full swing, and as usual, I had tuned them out. At some point, the conversation took on a more heated tone, and the intensity began to rise as my father and beloved Uncle Claude debated something that Grandmother had told these "grown men" to do. I have no idea how it got out of hand. Without warning, the discussion exploded into a full-blown argument between Grandmother, my biological father, and Uncle Claude. I don't think I'd ever witnessed a family screaming, yelling and cussing at one another like they were. But in the midst of the squabble, she suddenly remembered the turkey she had in the oven. She made a b-line from the dining room and stormed into the kitchen. I heard the oven door open and shut loudly with a clang, and as I turned toward the sound, I saw Grandmother hurling the charred black turkey across her pretty pink-painted kitchen as she screamed, "GET THE HELL OUT OF MY HOUSE!" I jumped up and ran into the kitchen. I snatched the phone receiver from the cradle hanging on the wall and called my mom, informing her that I was headed home. I grabbed my "nigger box," exited the house, and attempted once again to tune out all of the ROXBOROUGH madness. I rode that bus back down 16th Street, listening to Melvin Lindsey's Quiet Storm. It was one of the few things that could calm and soothe my mind in times of stress. As the bus got closer to home, I knew a real Thanksgiving dinner was waiting for me, prepared by my mom with love in our kitchen. When I walked into our apartment, I was greeted by the sweet aromas of honey-baked ham, a perfectly cooked turkey, mac and cheese, collard greens, potato salad, baked beans, and cornbread, and at that moment, I understood the last lines of Lucile Clifton's poem, "in the inner city." "*Or, like we call it, home.*"

I was troubled. After that Thanksgiving fiasco, I had no desire to visit Grandmother's house again. Yet, I still wanted to connect with her, to know her, and for her to get to know me. I decided to write her a letter and express my feelings and thoughts about what I viewed as inappropriate behavior. The letter was several pages long, and I had a lot to say. It was very respectful, with not even one curse word in it. It was simple and to point out. I shared how ashamed she should feel of herself for the constant emotional abuse. I hadn't taken my psychology course at Carroll yet, so I doubt that I actually used the phrase emotional abuse, but you know exactly what I meant. Something was definitely wrong with this woman. Her berating and verbal attacks on everyone had become unbearable. I signed the letter, folded it neatly, and placed it in the envelope. I made sure to use my best handwriting, then I licked the stamp and pressed it on the envelope. It was ready to mail. I felt a little tinge of apprehension when I dropped it in the mailbox, but I knew I had to speak up.

A few days later, Grandmother called. I was barely able to get "hello" off my lips before she attacked. "Erin, how dare you!" The venom in her words could not be dismissed. "I should've known you would write trash like this! You call this garbage writing!" Before I could respond, the dial tone told me she didn't care what I had to say. I only wanted to explain the emotional hurt that she was causing everyone, including me. Someone needed to do it! Interestingly enough, although I had basically spoken up for all the family members, that letter was held against me for decades by almost everyone in the Roxborough family. Thankfully, I had other adults in my life who were encouraging and positive influences.

As I was growing up, my mother would often say that I resembled her mother, Anna Mae Blair, in complexion, mannerisms, and attitude. She had been Eastern Star. Unfortunately, she passed away due to cerebral hemorrhaging when I was just a baby. I was so troubled as a kid that I'd often create imaginary conversations with my Grandma, Anna Mae. These conversations were the polar opposite of the real-life verbal exchanges with Grandmother. My conversations with Grandma Anna Mae were joyful and inspiring and resembled the relationships that my friends shared with their grandmas. In fact, I wrote many of them down as essays, dialogues, and poems. It was a thrill and a blessing to have one of the poems recited in a Carroll play by a close friend.

Dear Grandma,

You said to always remember my roots, my history, and I'll know my future… Well, I know of Tubman, Truth, Douglass, and King, and I still can't see no future for me! What do I have that nobody white don't have? Let me know, Grandma, What do you mean by hard work, initiative and persistence are the non-magic carpets to success? I do my work, I play ball, my friends are getting killed…And you say dreams are the key to success. What about my friend's dreams? He was smooth; he was gonna play ball. What you say?.......I can't go….Grandma, I got to be free. I'm getting older, you know the streets ain't for me, don't you trust me? Look, Grandma, I know how it is. Why you scared? God is Able, that is what you tell me…Man, this life ain't for me….I got dreams; if I'm ignorant, it's cause I haven't seen…I am bling; I need to see a better world. I ain't pressed; I just want success…I just want to be ….me.

When I turned 23, Grandmother gave me a copy of Gary Zukav's *Seat of the Soul*. I'm thinking; this is awesome, I can read it, soak it up, highlight key points, and then we could share our thoughts with one another. I was so excited to discuss the book with her. I just knew for sure this was the breakthrough in our relationship. We were going to create a bond and get over our communication barriers. I eagerly reached out to her over winter break from Syracuse, but instead of sipping tea and discussing our mutual aha moments from the book, I was scolded and condemned for what I had no idea. I attempted a few times but finally gave up. When she started her diatribe on all the things that weren't right about me and the world, I came up with an excuse and hung up the phone. I called my mother after every conversation with Grandmother. I needed her calmness after the emotional turmoil seemed to always that followed June. I did my best to keep in contact with Grandmother through my college years. I often called her just to check-in. But once she started in on my mother, I'd end the call before I got pissed off. I still wonder sometimes why I just never went straight the hell off on her.

It wasn't until I was an adult with my own children that Grandmother finally revealed to me that she had not graduated from high school, but she had married very well. I thought to myself, shit, that's why I suffered all the emotional abuse? Because she was jealous that I, her only granddaughter, had simply managed to excel academically and dare to even graduate and make something of my damn life? No wonder I lived in my head. Oh! But it didn't stop there; she went on to share in another conversation that she had a very strained and emotionally abusive relationship with her own mother. Ding! Ding! Ding! The alarms went off in my mind; it all made sense now why she resented my mother so and me to an extent. I had something she would never have, a close and loving relationship with my mother.

I remember calling her on Mother's Day in May of 2014. I had been thinking about her while my mom and I were shopping at JC Penney and Macy's. Grandmother's voice sounded a bit lighter and more upbeat than she ever had as far back as I could remember. She told me that she felt good because she had her two boys right there with her. It was one of our last conversations, but it was also the day we exchanged our very first "I love you."

Unfortunately, we weren't afforded more time to grow close; she passed away in November of that same year. We had reached a place of forgiveness and understanding. I loved her deep down, and I cried over the good memories we never really had together. Thinking about her no longer takes me to dark times or places. I found a way to glean some laughter and lessons from my early experiences with Grandmother. I can't help but chuckle when I think about how the former Jet Magazine cover girl could cuss you out on a whim or hurl a burnt turkey at your head to get her point across. Grandmother was hilarious in her own way. She had some deep scars from her own broken relationship with her mom, and Lord only knows what other trauma she may have endured. Although I would never know all of her history, her childhood dreams, and aspirations, I was able to piece together bits of her story in our last conversations. What was most important was that I now understood her pain... *HURT PEOPLE HURT PEOPLE.*

6

My Uncle Claude

Claude Roxborough Sr., ESQ., was an attorney by trade and an astute businessman. Uncle Claude obviously inherited his entrepreneurial spirit from generations of Roxboroughs before him. In his twenties, he partnered with two other industrious entrepreneurs and opened The Foxtrappe on R Street. The Foxtrappe was a private club that catered to an exclusive professional clientele that included athletes, doctors, politicians, lawyers, entertainers, and judges. Named after one of the names given to destination points on the underground railroad during slavery, the Foxtrappe was Uncle Claude's pride and joy. When it opened in 1975, it was a haven for DC's rising professional African American population who were often refused admittance to white clubs.

In addition to his ownership in The Foxtrappe, Uncle Claude began acquiring real estate in the early eighties. His expressed purpose for delving into real estate was to build and grow the Roxborough family enterprise. He successfully managed the properties for decades which provide cash flow income for Grandmother and enabled my father to house his dental practice rent-free for more than 30 years.

I don't know if there was some sort of unresolved sibling rivalry at play between my father and his brother. But it was the ownership and financial responsibility of the budding real estate empire that eventually drove a deep wedge between them. My father had relinquished his ownership in the property on Irving Street but wanted to continue enjoying the benefits of ownership along with free rent and no responsibility. You see, there was litigation against Uncle Claude over the family real estate holdings. The disagreements, accusations, manipulative marital relationships, unfulfilled promises, and Lord only knows what else went own between them, but it played out like a soap opera after Grandmother and Grandfather passed away. Uncle Claude begged his brother to cease litigation against his own family because he knew the growing tensions could inevitably destroy everything they had built.

One thing that was always apparent, despite the dysfunction, rivalry, and other challenges, Uncle Claude loved his family. He did all he could to ensure that the family remained unified.

He didn't differentiate; he loved and accepted his stepparents and me as full family members. Which meant if he could do anything to help you, he would. Shortly before his death, he had promised his stepmother, the first woman to serve as the director of the NAACP, that he would have the musical Detroit 1938 on Broadway within a year. He insisted that my biological father and his son join in and make those goals attainable.

Uncle Claude and I grew close in the years before his death. He constantly told me, "Erin, I may not have been the best attorney, but I am a damn good man." I wholeheartedly agree. We spent hours talking about my teenage, college, and graduate years. He even admitted how he had been detached and aloof during that time. He told me how sorry he was for that. Unlike others in the family, Uncle Claude dared to put forth an intentional effort to get to know me. We embraced each other with forgiveness and self-awareness of past missteps and acknowledged our role in the breakdown of our communication. Most of the strain in our relationship honestly had nothing to do with either of us.

Uncle Claude not only loved me, but he respected me. I remember his reaction when I shared with him how I'd felt when my dad declared," Erin, do you mean to tell me that the only thing you could think of was to become a teacher?" It was as if he had stabbed me in the heart. I was a disappointment to him. As if to reinforce his disdain for my career choice, my credentials were deliberatively omitted from my grandfather's and grandmother's obituaries. *Letters never actually matter at particular times, right?*

But dear ol' Uncle Claude stepped up and lovingly showed how proud he was of me by making it a point to acknowledge the letters behind my name. His actions signaled to the rest of the family that the M.S. and M.Ed. that I earned were no less important or significant than their MDs and JDs. He accepted me for who I was, who I wanted to be, and who I had become.

When I told him that I had forgiven the absence and emotional abuse from his brother, he was shocked. He asked me to pray for him and not give up on him. I agreed out of love and respect for my uncle, but I had to admit that it wasn't an easy task. The mere fact that I had spent about 30 years begging and desiring that man's love and acceptance really concerned me. It felt it was insane for me to keep searching for validation and acceptance from him, but *every little girl deserves and desires to be loved by her daddy.*

The Uncle Claude I came to know was flamboyant, exuding with life and wisdom. He had this habit of making funny facial expressions that matched his often-silly moods, and laughter followed every interaction with him. Whenever he wanted to talk to me about serious topics, he would always begin with a parable to focus on something he wanted me to learn first.

Shortly after Grandmother's death, he invited me to come by her house to "help him." He gave me a key to her house and let me know that I was welcome there anytime. I saw it as an opportunity to make up for all the years we'd lost. I began to visit him regularly and helped out by cleaning the house. Every time I stopped by the house, I'd find the cutest little cards on the table with words of encouragement just for me. I believe he wanted to create the happy memories that we should have had there, and I was determined to help him do it.

I'd also get these random text messages, "Woman, get over there. I left some things for you." I'd get to the house, and there would be one of the cards with a little pocket money for the twins and one of his signature funny sayings inside. I'd just stand there and smile. I had longed for that kind of relationship with my dad for most of my life. Uncle Claude was part of the reason I had never given up trying to make that happen. Sitting with him at that table in that pink kitchen was the only sign of life, joy, and happiness I could remember ever having in that house.

In our time together, I learned so much about who he was as a man and how he saw the world. He wanted to leave a legacy. He was aggressive in the most protective and loving way over the family's children. When he acknowledged me as an heir at law of the family, it was his intent that I would be included in the family business. He wanted the family to come together in solidarity, and he demanded that everyone should be taken care of and share in the benefits of having been born a Roxborough.

At one point, he wrote a letter informing everyone that alcoholism is a family curse and that my biological dad's recent DWI arrest should be a starting point for dealing with and working with his depression. As a recovering alcoholic since 1972, Uncle Claude modeled for everyone that you didn't have to be ashamed or embarrassed about it. He was a man with humility and integrity. He wanted to help others, and he worked tirelessly to do that. Hell, he started by trying to heal his own family. *How can anyone not respect and admire that?*

I developed a deep respect and admiration for my uncle. He was keenly aware of his vices and his storied past. He would make jokes about my casual drinking and send little teasing yet caring texts on a Friday if I was heading to a happy hour. He'd remind me not to drink too much, "You know you're a Roxborough, right?" It was these things and so much more that made it so easy to love him.

In 2014, a family meeting of the Roxboroughs was held to discuss the ongoing plan and purposes of holding the property at Irving Street NW and Georgia Ave. It was agreed that the property should never be sold and that the property had been given to the family for the purpose of securing the future education and development of the family and the children of Claude and John Roxborough and their grandchildren. The plan as stated in a letter from Uncle Claude was for my half-brother to receive the benefits of the cashflow from the rental property while attending medical school, and then I was to begin receiving the rental income to help support my daughters' high school and college educations.

I do not now, nor have I ever received, one penny from any rental income from the property that was once my biological father's dental office. I used to drive past his office on Georgia Ave and Irving Street NW almost every week while on my routes from St. Augustine. It never failed. Every time I came near that building, my mind wandered. I'd find myself imagining what it would be like to stop in just to say, "Hi, Dad, how's your day going?" or drop in to surprise him for a daddy-daughter lunch date. Of course, I never did any of that. There was that one time I visited when I was around 23. There was a slight misunderstanding while attending my cousin's graduation from Columbia Law School. My father approached out of the blue and said, "Hey, I'll take you home." Anger welled inside me, and I replied, "I'll get home the same way I got here." I turned around and left. Uncle Claude followed me out to the street as I hailed a cab. He tried to convince me to stay, but I didn't have it. I got in the cab and returned to the bus just as I had come. In hindsight, I now realize that perhaps that was my father's attempt to connect with me. But in my mind, I couldn't trust it or him because I didn't know.

I wanted a relationship with my father, and Uncle Claude understood that. I believe that if there was anyone who could have made it happen, it would've been him.

He wrote a letter, attached it to an email, and copied it to the entire family. He directly expressed that he believed that his brother had time to get to know his wonderful granddaughters and me. He encouraged my father to take advantage of the time while he was still on earth. I couldn't have agreed more. When I received that letter, it warmed my heart that someone believed in me and saw my value.

I made my last attempt at Christmas 2019. While sitting in church one Sunday, I was inspired by Father Pat's sermon. I decided to reach out to my father, and I was terrified. He was abrasive and quick-tempered, and he had made me feel so unworthy all of my life. I resolved myself to give it one more try; with thoughts of Uncle Claude cheering me on I made the phone call. When answered, I channeled every ounce of bravado and cheer that I could, "Hey, Dad, it's me, Erin. How would you like me to treat you to a cup of coffee?"

"Erin, do not ever call me again." The phone clicked with finality. My heart pounded against my chest as if it would explode at my next breath. The beeping of the phone line shook me out of the stupor I'd just been cast into. I swiped to answer; it was one of my very best friends, Daryll Butler. Through tears of anguish and sorrow, I relayed what had just occurred with the man who had, for the very last time, confirmed that he had no soul or heart. I could hear the anger underneath Daryll's words, "Hey, let's go to Cooper's Hawk for a few drinks. E. I got you…"

Did I mention how happy and appreciative I am for Uncle Claude loving us? I will forever be just as loud and crazy about him as he was while sitting in the St. Augustine school auditorium, yelling out, "Those are my grandnieces!"

I would do absolutely anything to be able to press the rewind button on joyful memories that should have been woven throughout my childhood. I wish I had more memories to place in this book to go back and revisit and read as often as my heart desired. A place where our memories overflowed, just like our love for him.

His great intentions for me died along with him in November 2016. I don't get to have one penny, nor a dime, from the Roxborough legacy as my uncle and Grandmother desired. My biological dad made sure of that. The detailed plan that Uncle Claude put in place was not honored. I'm speaking specifically about the profits from the property on Irving Street.

Uncle Claude would always say, "It's about the children." At this point in my life, there's absolutely nothing else my dad could ever do to hurt me again. It is my prayer that my daughters can and will continue to keep their relationships with their biological uncle.

If I just sit here for a moment, I can hear Uncle Claude right now, "Damn, girl, you're extremely intelligent. You remind me of my son, but just remember, I am the coolest out of all…. Yep, he sure was.

7

My Syracuse Days

In the fall of 1992, I entered Syracuse University as a freshman. I was excited and apprehensive about this new chapter in my life. I was born and raised in D.C. Syracuse was upstate New York; it seemed like another world. Before the fall semester began, new students were invited to the campus for orientation to get a glimpse into this world of higher education. During one of the orientation sessions, the presenters shared a few demographics about the city of Syracuse. They made a point to warn us not to venture "under the bridge." The fear-mongering to stay away served to perpetuate the stigma of Pioneer Homes, a low-income housing project, as a danger. These kinds of conversations became a lightning rod to inspiring me to think of magical ways to give back to my community. Of course, a few of my new friends and I ventured under the bridge a few hours after that. Our little trip to the wild side turned out to be simply good exercise. According to what we had been told, we expected to see loads of people hanging outside, lurking around corners, waiting to pounce on unsuspecting students like us. To our surprise, the housing projects deemed so dangerous turned out to be not so dangerous at all. As a matter of fact, at that time, the crime rate in that particular area of Syracuse was not high. It's amazing how perception works, isn't it?

Syracuse's orientation week also happened to include "Minority" weekend. You see, "Minority" weekend was…. That weekend stirred something in me. As you have already learned, I was a veracious reader growing up with an unusually strong interest in African American heritage and its global influence and impact. But that weekend, the little spark I'd carried all my life was ignited to become a social consciousness flame that continues today. I was exposed to so many organizations on the campus, many of which I eventually joined or became involved in some way.

It was Friday, the end of orientation week, and festivities were happening all over campus. I meandered about, checking out literally everything. There were flyers everywhere promoting fraternities, sororities, this party, and that party. As I stood peering at all party options for the weekend, trying to decide whether I would or would not venture out alone to either one of them, my thoughts were interrupted. "Hey, are you going to this underground party in the Schine Student Center tonight?"

"Ahh yeah, I guess," I replied, somewhat caught off guard. I turned to the tall young woman standing beside me. "I really don't know anybody, so I'll probably just end up standing on the wall listening to the music."

"I'm Sarah, Sarah Glover from Jersey," she chimed, a big grin lighting up her face.

"I'm Erin, born and raised in Washington D.C.," I replied, matching her grin with a Cheshire smile of my own. It was funny how we felt the need to let each other know where we were from. Maybe it was the fact that we were in this new world called Syracuse, away from all we knew. I'm not quite sure why but I felt an instant connection to Sarah.

"Do you have a roommate? I asked before I even thought about it. The words just flew out of my mouth.

"No, you?" She countered.

"Well, you have one now," I informed her.

That evening, Sarah and I ventured together to the party in the basement of Schine. As we made our way to the building, we could hear the Caribbean beats wafting through the walls into the cool night air, beckoning us to come inside. Now, I grew up surrounded by Caribbean music, and I'd developed a deep love for it through my babysitter Jean and other neighbors. In fact, a lot of my teen years involved me being lost in my own world—headphones on—old Caribbean sounds playing on my "ni***box." I knew the lyrics and the dialects of all my favorites. But that night was different. The sounds and rhythms were distinctive. It was a dancehall Reggae, and I loved it!

We could see the disco lights illuminated that packed basement in the Schine Student Center as we approached the entrance. Without warning, Sarah bellowed, "*Ting-a-ling, dancehall it swing, DJ head stuck up when hear boom riddim, Ting-a-ling a ling, school bell a ring, knife and fork ah fight fi dumplin. Booyaka! Booyaka! call for Shabba Rankin*!"

I couldn't help but laugh. Sarah got me hyped! You hear me? That was our first college party. The first of many, but by the second semester, we realized that we had to get a grip on our grades before the partying provided us with one-way tickets back to D.C. and Jersey, respectively.

Sarah, and I developed an awesome friendship that first year. I couldn't have asked for a better roommate. Sarah an aspiring journalist, was one of those people who seemed to have always known what she wanted to do. No matter where we went, she treated her camera like an American Express card—she never left the room without it! As I listened to my new college roommate share her love and awareness of her Jamaican roots, I began to listen and appreciate these first college encounters from a new perspective.

My freshman year at Syracuse was just the culture shock and exposure I needed, coming out of a predominantly Black Catholic Highschool. I embraced the newness of it all but still appreciated seeing a few familiar faces from home around campus, like star athletes George McDaniels,

Lawrence Moten, and Marvin Graves. I have fond members of George trying to cheat off my papers in Spanish class.

There is one very special person who journeyed from Archbishop Carroll to Syracuse along with me during freshman year. Daryll Butler is one of my very best friends. Daryll embraced me as a sister then and has continued to show up for me over the past 30 years. He's the one that knows exactly what to say to talk me off the ledge!

The energy of being in college excited me. I was always refreshed and ready for that long walk up all those hills across the quad. I pretty much lived in Byrd library. It felt like home, like my days spent in DC Public libraries growing up. I discovered I needed less sleep; I was eating right. I wanted to work out. I wanted a six-pack—I wanted to be fine as hell! I wanted to fight depression.

Everything was new. It was this new and intoxicating energy of self-discovery. We were a part of this culture. I was beginning to redefine myself. This was one of the greatest periods of my life.

I was grateful for the opportunity to lose myself in that world of Liberal Arts courses. Despite critics against college loans, I definitely do not harbor any deep regrets about seeking an education. My partial scholarship and student loans paid for my entire educational experience. Every student loan I have ever taken out is paid in full. I'm not a proponent of discouraging people from taking out loans, considering I came up with a financial plan to pay down my debt. Discipline was and is everything. I for damn sure didn't always have discipline. I had to damn near lose everything, but I was determined to get my shit back; I can tell you that much. Anyway, back to Syracuse!

During sophomore year, the activism in me blossomed. I joined the Student African American Society (SAS) and learned from Brother Agyei Tyehimba, who is now an educator, best-selling author, and a Black

Liberation Coach from Harlem. I also wrote for two campus publications, the Black Voice and Daughters of Kush. The Daughters of Kush was an African- centered sisterhood rooted in the spiritual and intellectual study of the Afrikan experience. This organization's focus was on developing deeper self-awareness and self-actualization based on self-love. It was an amazing experience. My eyes were already open to feminist works, and I delved into a deeper study of some writers that I was only slightly familiar with, like, Audre Lorde, Patricia Hill Collins, and a host of poets. It was amazing to see the diversity on our campus, and I became so empowered by reading Paulo Friere's, *Pedagogy of the Oppressed*. This book really shaped my identity at the time and inspired me more.

My undergrad years were a time of soul-searching for me. I remember in one of my philosophy 187 classes, a student wrote an editorial bashing a speaker Khalid Muhammad from the Nation of Islam, who had been invited by the Student African American Society. It wasn't so much that I disagreed with my classmate altogether because I did my best to be open-minded. Still, when his editorial suggested that Black people were inferior, I was livid! This was around the same time that Charles Murray and Richard Herrnstein published *The Bell Curve*. I recall expressing my frustration and angst to my mother, and she matter-factly told me, "Yes, you can be a little radical just do it after you've earned the right GPA." You got to love her; no matter what, she always reminded me that my education was my priority!

Actually, I wasn't as vocal as most of the people I knew. I surrounded myself with people committed to fighting racial biases, especially since we were being confronted by Eurocentric paradigms, attitudes, and classroom behavior which put us forever on the defense. I think I was afraid to speak up about particular issues because I didn't want to be labeled as the "angry Black girl." So, I decided to put my pen to paper; it seemed like the safer outlet at the time. I wrote an editorial response letter in the

Daily Orange, the university's student newspaper. I channeled some of my utter shock and dismay at classmates for their support of Murray and Herrnstein's book, their overall arrogance, and the professor's inability to guide the classroom discussions in a productive way. We were supposed to be discussing Aristotle, Plato, and Socrates, and there were days when the discussions would go so far off the map that I wondered if the professor even had a lesson plan. I was one of two Black people in the class, and it got old quickly, as it did for most of my college friends, having to be the spokesperson for Black America.

I was relieved to meet a few good whites, liberal-minded friends, primarily young women who were also angered by the savage inequalities that affected marginalized black and brown communities. There were two dynamic sister-friends who were influential as I began raising my voice for Black America. "Dirty Jersey," Keisha Campbell, Jamaican born, super intelligent SAS member would drive me to some of the areas in New Jersey mentioned in Jonathan Kozol's Savage Inequalities. And there was Qiana Williams, born and raised in Syracuse, they were pretty vocal about inequality and racial disparities themselves.

I had a real "Karen" in my life long before the name became a pejorative. She was my professor in the School of Education and was life-changing. We often met for coffee to discuss race, and I shared my passion for Patricia Hill Collins, Black Feminist Thought. She gifted me with Audre Lorde titles, and we would talk for hours.

The writer Sonia Sanchez wrote, "The saner you become, the more mad you're made to appear." This was the beginning of my journey toward becoming more aware of feminist ideas. Although I had both black and white friends, I never felt insecure about my sexuality or anyone else's. *Why is it that people tend to assume that just because you want to learn about feminist ideals, you must be lesbian*? Yep, just one more thing to discriminate against.

Who the hell cares about what anyone else is doing in their bedroom? My advisor had that Ellen DeGeneres vibe and personality, and yes, she was Lesbian. She had this ability to rip into people about their racial bigotry that was absolutely awe-inspiring. I so enjoyed watching her go to work on anyone demonstrating racist behaviors. There were so many anti-racist people in my world, but unfortunately, there was also racism on campus. I would be foolish not to admit that.

Despite everything, I stand by my decision to attend Syracuse University. It was one of the best decisions I've ever made. The faculty in the African American Studies department and the School of Education were like family to us, and when they lectured, we listened attentively. Doing well in these classes truly changed my perception of myself. Qiana and I would spend hours talking about identity and the impact of her blended heritage, having a white mother (Italian Irish) and a Black and Native American Creek Indigenous father. It's W.E.B.'s theory of "Double consciousness," having to live in two worlds, one Black and one White. I had become adept at living in two worlds from around the age of nine. It was a necessity in order to maintain my sanity. My journaling was a source of freedom and reflection for me. It was my lifeline. I knew that if I were to survive this marginalized living, I had to start expressing or better yet releasing some of all the stuff that was beginning to clog my spirit and soul. Around this time, I started transcribing all my childhood writings onto floppy disks. I know that makes me "old," according to my twins. I would sit in the computer lab for hours, going through notebook after notebook, typing every word into the computer. And then, it hit me, I was going to break out of my shell and start sharing my writings.

I've always admired the talent of all of my college friends to this day, and there wasn't a soul who could tell us anything about who we were or who we would become. Here is one of my writings from my Syracuse days.

8

Creativity

Just because I am oppressed does not mean that I am depressed, obsessed with your twisted lies that serve to suppress and repress my divine image,

I am creativity…. Black woman from antiquity All colors that are, come from me

I am the original statue of liberty All praises due should be for me

If it were not for me you would not be. I am the sustainer of life, the Sycamore tree and the sistrum shaking up the world for the reconstruction of herstory.

On my earth, there's understanding A clear picture of Ma'at, truth, justice and righteousness, With this,

I never rot

I am born, reborn through infinity I never die I am life through the souls of Black folk in us and in the sky.

Just because I am oppressed And the Caged Bird sings in her nest about the rape of a people, our history erased, downtrodden, beaten, and despised. We are no four-footed beasts If you must die, it will not be us. We are creativity…

We are what we must

9

With This Faith

I've got this faith that has a tendency to drift

However, when immobile, it brings harmony to my soul & if I can only keep safe its vigor

I believe my life's disappointments can grow old.

For all of the steady reoccurrences of blood spattered on my heart, rejected by people who should have known better

This faith has adorned me with two precious jewels, Arianna and Alanna

Mommy's sweet baby girls to cherish forever

I've never been enticed by the world's riches

Holding onto painful memories, I walked alone

Away from the superficial

Growing up the only child

I preferred to

Just be

Deep within

From what was hip, I set my own trend

And made the time to become a good friend

Just to learn, even though distant, that I only have a few

All I've ever really needed to get me through

My situation

From age 10 to 21, it seemed I searched submerged in this loner reality

Of, "Where is my family?"

Was this a plot?

A daddy's maybe not

My hard-working mother's 12-hour shifts several times weekly

Assisted me in earning my academic degrees- unselfishly

I realized in my twenties that there is just truly no need for pity

That my life is really beautiful

One nurture in my surrounding plot

Has proven plentiful

I teach because I believe in sunflowers

With standing stems of knowledge

I also believe in building those monumental

Memories of good

Conversations

In college

With all that, I believe

I've got this faith that sometimes has a tendency to drift

However, when immobile, it brings harmony to my soul & if I can only keep safe its vigor

I believe

My life's wild disappointments can grow old.

If I only knew what I know today

As those of wisdom often say

That my faith, as promised, is reaping

Restoring my joyful years that the Locust has eaten......

I'd probably just shove ahead, drudging only those useless memories of my past—

And just write a poem for those I love deeply

Living in love as long as I can last

With this faith

(Written on July 16, 2005)

10

I Think I'll Wear More Dresses from Now On

There are a few things that I've determined to impress upon my daughters as they grow into the beautiful, educated, and independent young women I know they will be. I need them to believe and have faith that God in heaven is the only Father that they can truly depend on. Their earthly father is prone to fallibility—like all of us—however, his inability to hold them in a safe space and nurture them has absolutely nothing to do with them! I want them to know that the enduring faith in our Heavenly Father is abundantly more than enough to heal, help and protect their hearts, minds, and souls, and for some of us, He is the only Father we've ever had.

It's my prayer that their superficial relationship with their father will change and deepen as they grow older. I am truly *not* a woman who doesn't want their child to have a loving and strong relationship with their father. Despite a person's intentions, their actions and the consistency thereof demonstrate the health and sincerity of their love for others and themselves. Though many are accused, there's no woman or man that can truly rob another parent of their "parental rights," what actually happens is that they abdicate those rights. Some people just don't show up.

My husband had been MIA. Neglect seemed to be his middle name. The responsibilities and burdens of our family and home fell solely upon me. I felt like I was the man of the house. No wonder I tended to wear pants all the time. And no, this is not some anti-feminist attitude; it reflects the reality of a woman married to a man who was not holding up his end of the agreement. And hell, yes! I had a right to expect that he would love me, take care of me, and support me emotionally, financially, spiritually and in every other way that I needed, just as I did for him—that is marriage.

For years, my weekly Things-To-Do list roadmap in my fight to maintain my mental health despite a divorce from an irresponsible dude. It's time for me to switch to the other side of my Gemini personality. "Hold ya mule," as my favorite Vegan actress, Tabitha Brown, always says. Thought I'd share a few snippets of my journaling from that time, so ya'll see where my mind was.

Mon, Sept. 8, 2008

Dear Diary:

"Shit, I need some damn structure and stability," I thought to myself. For the last month, I've developed and maintained a routine for myself and my twins. It is my hope that I am successful at selling this marital house. Once I'm home from work, 8pm: M-(read 30 mins) T: Meal Prep. W-bible study Th-contact realtor Fr=Movie night with my twins. Last night, I had to get to bed at 8pm. Totally exhausted. It was a long Monday because I had to buy 2 new back tires. I missed the "P" team meeting on the French side. I got homework done with the twins, practiced writing their names, read Llama, Llama, and practiced this week's spelling words.

Sept. 12th, 2008

Dear Diary:

Well, I had to fax the release form back. No sale. Their dad is supposed to be getting a better part-time job, according to him. How long has it been since he's seen his twins? I can't even recall. That's a damn shame. A sin and a shame.

Accomplishments: Sent hardship letters to 3 credit bureaus and emails to dllr.state.md. us. Gotta help myself. Good news. I should be receiving my salary plus retro pay. Damn, I am glad I got this Pupil Personnel Worker position.

Sept. 29th, 2008

Their dad hasn't been around for months. Not a penny from him either. Mental note: stay on my healthy habits, gotta use my affirmations more. Gotta put into life. Gotta keep it up.

Dec. 2, 2008

All last month had been pure hell. Resolved. The past is the past. F it. I am obtaining an absolute divorce by internet. (Thankful for friends with helpful tips) I am not paying any lawyer thousands of dollars. F that. I can do this s*** my damn self. (minus fees for the required mediation, etc.) I'm getting a divorce so that I can get my excellent name back again. Shit, I gotta get me back. Maybe if I can get him to sign and agree to pay $400-600 a month, I won't push for child support. Please make him be responsible. Please, Lord, Yes, I will give him till end of Dec to see if he will mess this up. ...I mailed a promissory note to my sister n law, Lanae. I am doing my best to obtain and retrieve my money.

I felt myself slipping further and further into depression as I was getting much closer to the divorce process.

Sarah, my SU roommate, was visiting D.C. for one of her many workshops or media conferences, I can't remember which, but we made plans to meet. While we were sitting in a diner chatting, Sarah mentioned something she'd seen on Facebook. I casually mentioned that I wasn't on Facebook.

"Erin, what do you mean you don't have Facebook? Come on, create an account, get with it, Girl!" She chuckled in disbelief. Yep, just one more thing that made me almost embarrassingly archaic and stuck in the past, holding to my floppy disks and CDs.

I contemplated creating a Facebook account for a little while because I was so ashamed that my personal life was in complete shambles. Finally, in early 2009 I took the leap. I sat up late one night, searching and hitting up every friend's friend list, click add, click add. As I clicked and added, I reminisced on fond memories and old friends. I couldn't avoid my feelings of failure in my marriage and life, but I said to hell with it; I needed to reconnect and hang out with people who reminded me of joyful things. It was a good decision. I reconnected with so many old friends, including Warren Mayo and Derek McNeil, and a few others. These Carroll guys stepped up and helped out this newly single mother with whatever I needed, and they didn't ask for anything in return. They helped to make my journey as a single parent a lot less stressful. My twins have the absolute best God-father ever who has helped me a countless number of times. Marcus Walker, a Carroll alum, is the best God-father ever to my twins and my gratitude for my Carroll classmates run deep.

A few days later I went shopping and picked a sexy new dress!

11

The Beginning and the End

It was me. I was the one who initiated the legal separation and the divorce, not him. Just one year before the divorce, my ex had been declaring his undying love to me. Nah, he was declaring his devotion to my bank account and credit cards. The only reason I had delayed leaving him was simply due to the demise of his father.

His father had been an admirable and highly respected man. He graduated from Howard University and had an esteemed reputation as the Director of Public Works in a neighboring city. He'd always shown me kindness and respect. I smile when I think of how he would always offer to bring bulk food to *our* house whenever he went shopping at Costco. He stepped in to save the day for me many times when I was struggling to make ends meet toward the end of our marriage.

Pop-Pop would have been a remarkable grandfather to my twins. I really wish they could have known him. I'll always cherish him. He was a good man. May his soul rest in peace.

My husband had grown up in a middle-class two-parent household along with his brother, sister, and dog. They had a present father, who had been instrumental in getting them jobs. They lived a relatively comfortable life. I figured since at least one of us had been raised in a typical two-parent family, the odds were in our favor to last forever. Hmph!

I thought that I was missing something growing up in a single-parent household. Well, fucking realistically, I did! I was missing a damn father...

brother…sister…aunt, and uncle! I don't really remember whether they had a dog and the proverbial white picket fence growing up, but I do know that he had an abundance of self-centeredness and self-pity, which seemed to be major themes in his life.

We started out as an urban American love story. Girl meets boy at happy hour in a nightclub called DREAM. Who would have imagined that it would lead to a nightmare? It was 2002, and I had just come back from vacationing in San Juan, Puerto Rico. I was probably feeling myself, you know, sporting a fresh tan and a fly outfit. As we used to say back in the day, I had it going on. And yes, the fellas were jockin' ya girl, lol! Anyway, when Dude (that's how I'll reference him from this point on) approached me, his swagger was on point because he captured my attention. The thing is, he wasn't even my damn type. Don't get me wrong, he was attractive, but I prefer the more melanated brothers; *I know that's not a word*! But you know exactly what I'm talking about. There's nothing more beautiful than a tall dark chocolate brutha with a bald head! Can I get an amen! Anyhoo, Dude was charming and attentive, just what every woman wants. We became an item pretty quickly. As we spent time together over the following months, I found myself confiding to him how not having my dad in my life had affected me. He listened and comforted me. He bought me nice things and surprised me with little gifts here and there. I found myself falling hard. I felt safe when I was with him. He shared his aspirations and dreams of opening a business, and I co-signed on the promise of that future. I believed in him and wanted to help him build that dream.

At some point, we decided to move in together, a sensible plan considering we were in love and we could save on expenses living in the same household. I assumed that we operated under similar middle-class values that my mother instilled in me—work hard, manage your money, take care of your responsibilities, and save. After we moved in together, I began to notice some things. He was really bad at managing his finances and would go to his father for help a lot. I didn't have the option of going to my father for any kind of help as a kid or as an adult, so I reasoned that this was a sign of a good relationship. A father helping his son realize his dreams.

In December 2003, I purchased my very first home in Waldorf, Maryland. Growing up, I didn't have much, but I accomplished it with determination. I paid my mortgage on time every month, like clockwork. And yes, Dude moved into the new house with me.

We got married on August 8, 2004. Like a dutiful wife reared in the Catholic tradition, I added my new husband's name to the title. I wasn't concerned about his financial management skills *'cause we were married and in love*. Like the dutiful husband I believed him to be, he agreed to assume responsibility for the loan on our home. Perhaps, that was one of my first mistakes. I didn't know any better. How does the old saying go, "When you know better, you do better!"

Not long after our wedding, I discovered that I was pregnant. We were thrilled to become parents. Our daughters were born on March 16, 2005. As I reflect on this time, I realize that I still carry some hurt. You see after the twins were born, I experienced for the first time what I had believed my marriage would be like from the beginning. It was beautiful. Dude took very good care of me. While I recuperated from my c-section, he made sure I got up frequently to walk as the doctor had instructed. He changed diapers, prepared bottles, bathed, and dressed the twins. He cooked and cleaned and ensured that I got the rest that I needed. At one point, he moved my mom in to help out as well. I suspected that it was so she would take the load off of him; *I can't prove it in a court of law,* but I appreciated having my mom with us. For one whole year, Dude was the epitome of a good husband. Then things started to fall apart.

Dude started bouncing from one job to the next. Now mind you, all his job hopping wasn't bringing in more income into the house but his spending habits were definitely bringing in more bills. As a matter of fact, it got to a point where my income was the only consistent money to pay the bills. I had been bamboozled! I guess I should have taken the clue when I realized just how frequently my father-in-law allowed his adult son to use his credit cards. *I mean, what grown man lets his daddy pay his bills?* The same kind that watches his wife support the family financially while he sits back and revels in the fruits of *her* labor. I had co-signed car loans for expensive boy-toys just so "my man" could flex and feel like or rather look like he as the man of the house. While I was working hard taking care of his children and his home, he was out doing who knows what without any concern for our welfare. *What the hell was I thinking when I said "I do" to this dude?* I would have come out a HELL of a lot cheaper with a "baby daddy!"

As time went on, our financial situation got worse. I took out a second mortgage to consolidate "our" debt. At one point, even his uncle was contributing more to our household than my husband actually was. I'll always appreciate his Uncle Carlton, *not his real name.* On several occasions, Uncle Carlton sent me money to pay the mortgage on our marital house. He was such a kind man who seemed to not be bothered by my ranting about his nephew's inability to be responsible and do provider-type shit. I was no stranger to family dysfunction, but damn!

Even after getting a loan modification, I struggled to keep up with my mortgage payments. I simply couldn't afford to raise two children without child support (at the time) and keep up with two mortgage payments on the house. I sought legal counsel. I decided to file for bankruptcy due to lawsuits from the second mortgage company coming after ME. My meeting with the creditors was on Thursday, May 14, 2009.

I was completely devastated. I kept thinking *so much for all the perfect attendance and great GPAs of my past.* I had never entertained thoughts of being a failure. Shit, I rarely wanted people to know just how depressed I was. I've always despised pity, and self-pity is even worse!! I'm good, though; did I point out that I have no assault charges? That was the benchmark I set for myself. If I can get through all of the BS without assaulting anyone…I'm good! LOL.

One day not too long after the divorce was finalized, I was playing around on Facebook. It was July 6th, Dude's birthday. I'm not sure what prompted me to search for him, maybe it was Facebook, me feeling melancholy or just being plain nosy, I'm not sure which, but I did. As I perused his profile, I came across wedding pictures! Upon future inspection, I discovered that this @!!*#&*!! got married seven days after our divorce was final! He married some chick who lived in District Heights, Maryland. I was livid! This @!!*#&*!!, was probably cheating on me this whole time! I called a friend who is an undercover cop and asked her to look this woman up and tell me what she could find. She told me that the woman had one or two DUIs. I'm not sure why hearing that calmed me. I have truly never felt superior to any damn body, but I needed to know that. I needed to know more about this woman who had apparently just become my twins' new stepmother. I still believe that the $1000 I deposited into his checking account the week of our divorce was used for that wedding. He swore to me he used the money for other purposes. Either way, why was I still supporting him financially? That's the reason my crazy ass should've been in therapy somewhere.

I remember stalking both of them on Facebook only to find pictures of our twins that I'd sent him posted all online. I was so angry I posted a message to let all his "fakebook friends" know that he is a person who rarely sees his kids. In fact, in my mind, he was the photo opt dad who posed for the camera to show his love and then disappeared for the other 364 days of the calendar year. Yep. I wish this wasn't my story, but it is. I also messaged the new wife. The message read: "Hello, I am sure you know who I am; I am just finding out about you." She replied and said something like, "he was hers, and she would see to it that he sends money to our twin daughters, and that they're gonna make plans to try to send some money to me soon." Shortly after that message, I sent her a message with her address and DUI information and pointed out that I had left him and that she had my leftovers. Shit, I know I was a nerd growing up, but I did have a lil' gangster come out of me then. I mean, seriously, I came at her respectively. How many people can do that? She immediately took down her Facebook account, and so did he.

Looking back, I couldn't help but think that he simply found another woman to "take care of him."

I wondered why it had taken him so long to leave the house. Yes, I did leave our marital house first. I didn't want to continue exposing our twins to bitter arguments. Long before I left, I'd give him money for the bills but the money went elsewhere. I recall our divorce mediator asking Dude if he did drugs when he couldn't explain where all of his money went.

Lionel was a source of comfort and reassurance for me around this time. He was right there when I happened upon evidence of Dude's newly wedded bliss. He reminded me that I had earned two master's degrees, attended Catholic schools K-12, and I'd never been arrested.

After everything I went through in my marriage, I totally understand how people get caught up with assault charges; I really do. At any rate, at that point in my life, I refused to continue begging for what should have been willingly provided. I simply could not convince myself to remain with a man who mirrored the same emotional and mental absence of my biological father. A father's role is to teach daughters the characteristics of a good man and demonstrate how they should be treated by men. I missed the boat on that one. How about daughters need healthy and present fathers? That sounds better. I needed to commit to therapy, and I had to reflect on some hard facts.

First, I searched and found an email just to validate that I had moved on and attempted to extend the "olive branch" to my ex-husband. You see why you don't want to play with intelligent women. We save journals, diaries, past emails, receipts, etc.

Jan. 31, 2016: My email to their dad read.

Good morning and Happy New Year, and I hope all is well with you and your family. I need to talk with you when you can. It's about the twins. It is my belief that by the time they are teenagers, the amount of expenses that I currently spend on them will only double. The number of child support that I am elected to receive through the courts since our divorce in 2009 is $1093.00 each month. I don't know if you remember, but in 2013 - I asked you if you would begin providing at least anywhere from $100- $200 in addition to the child support. At that time, I managed to keep both twins in their Catholic school, and I am very happy that they've been in Catholic school. I wish that you would agree with me and understand why I am asking that you begin to help me as you do know that every penny of the child support has gone to their school tuition. As I stated to you in 2013, most of the child support goes towards the school tuition, and I remember your mom would mail sporadic checks here and there, but it is not consistent enough to help with providing for clothing and accessories so I decided to reach out to you again to ask that you would consider changing your mind to consistently support them by providing some kind of money by the end of each month. I could plan to share with you where the money will go each month if that would make you change your mind or feel more comfortable.

There is no need for me to include the entire email. Do you think that he kept his promise? You guessed it. He did not. That was five years ago. Today is April 3rd, 2021. I'm glad you're following along here. I just stopped asking and begging, and I took the responsibility upon myself. It has never been the responsibility of my ex-husband's mother to support us financially, but I am grateful for the holiday money and cards she sends the twins every year.

I wasn't fortunate to have the proverbial affectionate and adoring grandma in Grandmother. My twins have both of them. I will continue to teach them to show gratitude for their Grands. As for me, I think I've been doing a pretty good job of keeping my cool, and since you know my past, then I hope that you would agree that I deserve some credit.

I'm forever grateful for my entire village. An integral part of that village is my godparents. Ironically, my Godmother's 69th birthday was the day I decided to pick up this writing, and the very next day, April 1st, was my Godfather's birthday. My Godfather sends me the most beautiful text messages and positive memes daily. They never fail to brighten my day. My godbrother was a godsend. He volunteered to do carpool duty with the twins one day a week just so I could get a break. My mom and several others in my village stepped to support me and even challenge me on a few of my decisions. In fact, one of those decisions was enrolling my girls in the expensive Outreach Christian Academy in Clinton, Maryland, when I was already struggling to pay our regular living expenses, two mortgage loans, and daycare. Shit, I figured since they didn't have a good Daddy, then I needed to provide them an exceptional private education. I don't know who the hell I thought my already struggling financial self was, but I did it anyway. My attitude was, *I'll be damned if I'm not gonna fucken do it.* The repercussions of that decision only escalated my problems financially; I couldn't afford it mentally, I was overwhelmed, and emotionally, I was all over the place. On top of all of that, the house needed major improvements in order to put it on the market for a good asking price. This was all part of the buildup to losing our home. It happens to millions of Americans every day, but this isn't a "woe is me" story; I'm just telling it like it is. I was humble before, and now I am totally humbled. Ok, so, 2009 in short, foreclosure, bankruptcy, divorce, and laid off, in that exact order. My first therapy appointment it was in the Spring of 2013. I made a damn list of what in the hell we would tackle first.

One final thought:

Ladies, please hear me! Dating someone who is not, cannot, and/or will not sustain themselves financially IS NEVER WISE. Period.

12

As We Forgive Those Who
Trespass Against Us...

The first time I met her, Dude had taken me to meet his family. I had been looking forward to meeting and getting to know them. I mean, they were a whole family, a mom, a dad, and three children! I was excited and nervous at the same time. After the cursory introduction to the family, they all seemed to go back to what they had been doing before we had arrived. I sat on the sofa all alone, trying not to look uncomfortable. She was the only one who seemed to notice that I was still there. She plopped down beside me and sparked a conversation, and we talked for hours. From that moment, I was sold.

Lanae, that's what I'll call her, was Dude's younger sister. She was a student at the University of Maryland College Park. She and I connected on so many levels from that very first encounter. In fact, she reminded me of myself at her age, ambitious, energetic, and friendly. I started attending her college events and even helped her get financial aid when she entered Howard University as a graduate student.

After Dude and I married, Lanae and I grew even closer. I'd always wanted to be the big sis. If you recall, I was the surrogate older sibling to the kids in my neighborhood. Since she *was* family through marriage, I'd finally realized that dream. In no time fell back on my familiar habit of "taking care" of other people. I mean, that's what big sisters do, right? The more time I spent with her and the family, I realized that there were some issues there. I never figured out what it was exactly. I don't know whether it was a strained relationship with both her parents or just her mom or something else but she seemed to not be the favored sibling from what I witnessed. I did my best to stay out of my mother-in-law's lane. Despite my earlier efforts, I truly feel that she and I never connected. Even with my struggle of not always knowing when and how to set boundaries, I knew for sure that I was not going to get in the middle of their mess. Coming from the dysfunction of my paternal side, knew she needed a shoulder to lean on, and I wanted to be there for her. Besides, I wanted so badly to be a part of this family that I didn't want to do anything to jeopardize being embraced by them. I wanted to believe that I had married into the best family ever, one that would accept and love me. Although that never happened, I always remained respectful.

Lanae began sponsoring concerts on campus, and I did my best to support her. When she became overwhelmed trying to balance studying and extracurricular activities, I stepped up, as a good big sister should, and guided her on how to successfully navigate her studies and college life.

One semester, I recall her car broke down. I was pregnant with the twins, bloated, huge, but pushing along. I volunteered to drive her back and forth from her apartment in Laurel to Howard University for one full week. It was no big deal from my perspective, I was no stranger to driving up and down the beltway so driving from Georgia Avenue to Laurel and back for one week was truly nothing to me. I wanted to be helpful. Now when I look back, I realize that was a mistake on my part, and it was then that our relationship began to take a turn for the worse. I went from being an awesome big sister to an always-available ATM. It didn't happen all at once; it was gradual. One day she stopped by my job at Washington Science Math Technology Charter School during lunch. She was strapped for money and asked if I could help out, so we ran to the bank, and I pulled out cash for her.

When the twins were born Lanae was a huge help. She was excited about being a new auntie and pitched in to help. At that time, I had my husband, a deepening relationship with Lanae, and of course, my mom, whom I could always depend on. I had the strong support system that every new mother needs, especially one with twins.

Lanae was an awesome auntie to the twins. She spent lots of time with them. In fact, she was indispensable when I took a trip to Petersburg, Virginia, to visit her and my husband's grandmother. Their grandmother was getting up there in age, and I knew it would mean a lot to her to see them.

When we arrived, I was greeted by this tiny, frail warm-hearted woman offering me a freshly baked sweet potato pie. I chuckled when I thought of how she that reminded me of my own mother and her "love cakes." My husband had told me so stories of how he cherished spending summers with her. She was so sweet and welcoming, which was the polar opposite of most of their other family members, except for Lanae. It made me wonder if they were really related. Anyway, that was one of the happiest times in my marriage.

As time went on, I began to see another side of Lanae. She seemed to struggle with daily life's decisions. I loved my little sis,' and I wanted to help. So, when she got her first job after graduating, I paid for a rental car so she could get to and from work because she was having transportation problems again. She needed to make some extra money, so I referred her to Martin Pollak Project, a tutoring agency where I used to work. She would come to me and ask for my advice, and I felt honored. It never crossed my mind to ask why she didn't go to one of her brothers or her father. I know you're probably sitting there screaming at the page, like we sometimes do in the movies, "Erin, watch out! Can't you see it? There's a problem here. She's gonna get you! I know, I should have seen it coming, but I didn't. Almost every week, she comes to me with some kind of sob story, this happened, or that happened, and the last line of each one resulted in me going to the bank. While working at Washington Math Science school, I lent that girl $3,000 from my hard-earned savings.

It's funny how time can give you a clearer view of the past. Looking back, I can clearly see the dysfunction in the family. They did not know how to communicate. There was always some type of commotion going on because somebody misunderstood or said something that created havoc.

There was one time, Lanae was dating this guy. According to everything she told me about him, he was kind, supportive, and always doing nice things for her. Well, in a conversation with Lord only knows who, my husband was told that Lanae's boyfriend had allegedly tried to harm her physically. Dude got unnecessarily hyped up, grabbed his gun, and stormed out of the house. I ran out the door behind him, yelling, crying, and screaming. When that didn't seem to work, I threatened him. "If you want to ever see these twins, you need to take the gun back into the house and make a real phone call and find out what actually happened, not jump to conclusions.

This was the absolutely ONLY time I had ever used the kids to threaten my husband. I only intended to keep them out of harm's way. I hated drama and conflict. I prided myself on being the opposite. My marriage was already on the rocks at that point; I was beginning to suspect that Lanae didn't have the best intentions toward me, and as much as I tried to keep it all glued together, things just seemed to continue to unravel.

Eventually, Lanae got a good job in her Daddy's office working for the Governor. I guess this was the steady financial support she had been seeking. I know that she stopped asking me for money but what she did not do was pay me back. Oh, she agreed numerous times but never came through. Why she wouldn't just agree to the payment plan, stick to it, and pay it back? She knew my situation; Dude was not providing for his family. I had already been seeing less and less of him, week after week, and soon after, Lanae followed suit.

In January 2008, I did receive email correspondence from Lanae. It read:

1/18/2008

Hey…glad is all is well. I would love to spend time with my nieces at least once a month…I would rather not place a date on it as my schedule often changes because of school this semester or travel with work. I also have problem checking in once a week, whether it is a phone or email because it helps us to keep in touch with each other even with our ridiculously busy schedules. So agreed? It also might be nice to take the girls up to visit their grandmother one day a she needs that! As for the money, I owe you "$2900. Everything is a learning experience and I would much rather give the $3000.00 in its entirety. Even you have to put some aside for Arianna and Alanna or any other expenses that you may incur. I also feel as though I am helping out as well. Plus, you didn't give me "$1500. What's done is done. I am planning on giving you another payment next month after the 4th) (rent Is due) and then once my tax money comes, I hope to pay at least half if not the entire sum. Like you, I'd much rather this money stuff be over soon.

I have restructured how I deal with things in life….so our business is our business and I don't believe anything unless I hear it from the source!

Well. Gotta run, going to a meeting about one of our signature events called AIDS Watch and then off to a candidacy mtg at Howard! I will be in the library tomorrow and Sunday organizing my many folders I have laid out for my thesis. *sigh* I know you understand how it can be…my friends are angry because I am not going to the movies with them ….but ya know….thesis first! Hahaha

We'll' talk soon!

Love,

Lanae

I really wanted to believe every word in this email. I wanted to believe that I had not been bamboozled or taken advantage of. I wanted to believe that the sister-in-law that I loved would honor her word. There were countless miscommunications and one failed mediation attempt with the Anne Arundel Conflict Resolution Center on February 9th, 2009, due to her not showing up. I did absolutely everything in my power to avoid court. I began to think beyond my feelings of hurt and betrayal and started thinking that money was taken directly out of my twins' mouth, for food, and I filed a suit in small claims court.

See the following Court Docket for small claims court below….

District Court of Maryland: (Complaint $5000) Or under … I am a single parent of 4-year-old twins. I have been separated for 3 years without child support or support from him or his family. My house just foreclosed on and I had to file for bankruptcy due to failure to pay the second mortgage company. I receive no help from their father. Our divorce hearing date is May 18th; I have suffered emotional and mental hardship from this family. I simply need the amount owed to me to continue to provide for my girls as a single parent. I am decent. The Plaintiff claims: $2215

You should already suspect my best friend and attorney, Daryll (also known as DDB), represented me in my claim. He drove me to my court in the early am that day. My heart felt like the ball in a soccer game, stomped on, bruised, and battered. I was just hanging on by a limb. I was lifeless, zapped of any hopeful energy, but I held onto the prayer he and I prayed just before we entered the courtroom. While waiting for the proceedings to begin, I sat motionless, wondering if this was a glimpse of what the divorce hearing would be, the forecast was impending doom and gloom.

The hearing didn't last long at all. I brought the numerous letters I had mailed her asking, pleading, demanding that she repay me for the money had borrowed to court as evidence. But there was only one letter that she submitted to the court.

Shit! I had forgotten all about that letter. I had been distraught and irate over the situation with Lanae, and I shared it with a well-meaning pastor friend. She suggested that I write a letter forgiving the debt so that I could move on from the relationship. At some point, I had considered asking the pastor to write a letter articulating that it was her idea to write the letter "forgiving" Lanae's debt. The really sad part of this story is that Lanae knew the toll the situation had been on my mental health, but obviously, she didn't give a shit about how it was affecting her nieces or me.

I lost the case.

I still believe someone called in a favor for her that day simply because she worked for the governor. I was seething and defeated. DDB grabbed my hand firmly and walked me out of the court. I don't think either of us said much of anything for the remainder of that day. After that betrayal, it would be years until I tolerated being physically near her again.

With all of the drama of foreclosure, bankruptcy, a layoff, losing a court case, and the divorce, I was drained emotionally, mentally, physically, and spiritually. To add insult to injury, one evening, I was working on putting my financial life back together and checking my credit score, and I saw Lanae's apartment listed on my damn credit report! *Why in the hell was her apartment on my credit report?* I knew exactly why Dude's cars and such were there, considering I co-signed for him, but I had certainly not co-signed on an apartment for her. I couldn't believe it! This girl had used *my* credit to obtain a spot for herself. It was always a damn WOW factor with these people.

Let's press forward to either 2011, 2012, or 2013; I don't recall which specifically. I do know that during those years, I fought fiercely for my new life, re-inventing myself. I did a pretty damn good job of it too. I carried a briefcase with all the documentation proving that I was a new creation. I had tons of copies of my divorce decree, my new and old social security cards, the twin's birth certificates, and social security cards. I also had hardship letters just in case I needed to show proof of my new identity. I was determined to continue re-invent myself over and over again as necessary to shake off Dude and his family's bad juju. I remembered that young woman I discovered in college, and I decided to love her fiercely. I decided to love ME.

These are only a few of the nightmares that will forever stick with me. It's difficult to see along the blurred lines just who did more damage to me, my then-husband or then sister-in-law.

It was August 8th, like 2013 …zoom past all of the past drama, I was in 'rebuild my life mode, and I got a letter from Bank of America. Imagine my confusion, because it was for an account that I thought was closed in 2009 around the time of my divorce. I rarely had overdraft fees and certainly no leftover bank account balances. That was the way my ex handled and mishandled his business, so I had absolutely no idea what it could be.

I opened the envelope cautiously, and BOOM! It was a demand letter requiring me to pay the account balance of $800. It turned out that ol' Dude had not only kept "our account" open but this &#&%**$#@!#!!!! Added his new wife's name to it! Who the fuck does that! I know what you're thinking; how did I not get locked up?

There I was, four years after the divorce, and I was still paying for crap! *What the hell?* I still cannot wrap my mind around that day when my mother came with me to the bank payoff and closed the account. As a matter of fact, it was supposed to have been a shopping day, so the entire family was present when I exercised the final demon. I am glad that chapter is OVER. As my daughter, Ari would say, "LITERALLY!"

13

Teaching Days

Washington Math Science Technology

Have you ever wondered what keeps a teacher committed to the profession despite the notorious administrative red tape or less-than-stellar wages? Well, let me clue you in. Now, I can't speak for every teacher that has ever taught, but I can tell you my "why," and I'd bet that many of you who are teachers would agree with me.

I taught at Washington Math Science Technology (WMST) for seven whole years. During my tenure there, I met some of the most wonderful people, teachers, administrators, and, most importantly, the students. If I could mention each person by name, I would, but there was one person with whom I connected on a level that inspired me and enabled me to share my passion for learning in new ways. Dr. Marie Parfait taught me that teaching is an act of revolution.

I was privileged to team-teach with Dr. Parfait. A graduate of FAMU and a history teacher, she would stroll through the halls and command her classroom adorned in beautifully woven headwraps and Afrocentric accessories. She was an activist!

She and I had so much in common. We collaborated to leverage our passion for our heritage and our love of learning to create an environment that taught our students to know that events from our history were as relevant today as ever and that they had the power to question, challenge, and change the role of oppression, racism, and privilege played in maintaining the inequities and injustices in society. Luckily, we were given the freedom to incorporate our race conscious approach into our units. We often aligned our history and literature units to coincide so that our students would truly get a feel for the historical and literary time period.

This team teaching and collaboration was a dream come true. Our students discovered the world of Che Guevara, John Henrik Clarke, Cheikh Anta Dip, Kwame Nkrumah, and Huey P. Newton in history class. The bell would ring and they would travel to my class and experience William Andrew's *The African American Novel in the Age of Reaction (Three Classics)*, *The African American Classics* and the *Classic Slave Narratives*. Our approach empowered our students to think deeply and critically. We loved on our "troubled kids" the most. We held a sense of urgency to ensure that our students became familiar with every Freedom Fighter and come to a realization that there is much more about our history than the Middle Passage. We were really learning as much from them as they were from us. Together, we wanted to make sure our students were equipped and able to compete with their peers across the district. Those team-teaching collabs were the absolute best lessons ever! And even better were the days I received letters from students showing gratitude for helping them "straighten out their lives."

Anacostia

I will never forget the day I received a letter in the mail informing me that I had been hired as a Dean of Students at Anacostia. I was absolutely thrilled. I had come to a point in my career where I was looking for a more administrative role. One that would enable me to stretch professionally and develop new skills. I had already begun working on a second master's in school counseling, and I had loved my work as a Pupil Personnel Worker in PG County serving two different schools and their principals, so I decided administration was the logical next step.

I chuckle at the fact that they ran the routine criminal background check, and there was that question asking if "I had a felony or misdemeanor conviction." Believe it or not, that was one of the key things that motivated me to "stay in my lane" and be the "good girl" that my mom raised me to be in spite of the hell I was going through at the time. I had to take care of my twins, and that meant I had to work. Now, I don't hold any judgment toward women who have sought revenge after being scorned or hurt. Sometimes it's almost impossible not to seek revenge, but jailhouse blue, orange, or whatever would not have been a good look on me!

Instead of revenge, I buried myself in my career. I hid in my signature black suit, stealthily moving through each day like I was a panther. I was probably the weirdest dean any of my students or colleagues had ever come across. Most would consider my behavior odd, if not straight outright crazy. I used to place $10 and $20 bills in my desk drawer just to build trust with my students. Somedays, I would be in ministry mode; I was quick to pull out my little green Bible and read a scripture with a student. They knew I was nuts, LOL. But my "crazy" worked. Many of the coaches would encourage me and give me pats on the back. I remember one day, a colleague tapped me on the shoulder and whispered in my ear, "Dean, you're the one who stabilized this Charles Drew Academy." That one line was another stone in helping to restore my confidence and reassured me that I was operating in my purpose. How do I know this? Because I was providing them with stability while I was going through a Category 8 earthquake in my personal life. No one there had any idea I was going through a divorce, losing my house and my mind.

Saint Frances Academy

Some years after the foreclosure, bankruptcy, and divorce, I was still running from everything. My pride and the fear of "what others would think" held me captive and unable to heal. Yes, I have gone to therapy, and I strongly recommend it for anyone…but it only works if you remain committed to it. I stopped going after two sessions. It wasn't the therapist; it was me. I struggled with opening up and divulging "my business" even to a professional! I know, I know…*do as I advise…not as I did*. Believe you me, my decision to skip out on therapy prolonged my pain and anguish. So, what did I do? I had to figure out how to heal that troubled little girl in me on my own.

I began by focusing on the basic things, food, shelter, clothing, and saving. After moving out of the house, we lived with my mom for a while so that I could save enough to get a place of our own. I knew it wasn't necessary for us to get our own apartment, but I wanted the twins to have huge bedrooms for their bunk beds from IKEA. The twins and I would visit IKEA so much it felt like we lived there. IKEA was the spot I went to dream of being in a home again and happy with my twins. It inspired me to work even harder to get to a place where I could rent a new apartment for us. The other reason I worked so hard was that a part of me really needed to exercise that same sense of independence my mom was raised to have. I found an apartment nearby, and we moved around the corner to Mount Rainier, Maryland.

During the divorce, I had been forced to bounce around quite a few times, and I didn't want that instability to negatively affect my twins. So, I did what I could to provide some kind of consistency. I made certain that no matter where we lived or what school I found myself in, we had dinner at the table with my mom at least twice a week.

I made what I thought was a wise and strategic decision by accepting a position at St. Frances Academy in Baltimore. The role was created for me by the principal, Dr. Curtis Turner. Dr. Turner had been the VP of WMST, my former supervisor, mentor, and friend. The position offered me a challenge, and I knew somehow that it would be worth it. It became the joy of my life to work in this inner-city Catholic high school, where I received some of the healing I needed.

My work schedule was absolutely beautiful because my morning block was also my planning period which allowed me to get the twins to school by 7am, and I then would catch the 7:20am or 7:30am MARC train. The train would pull into Penn Station by 8:30am, and from there, it was a 15 min walk to the school on Chase Street, rain, sleet, or snow.

That daily commute on the MARC, back and forth from Union Station to Penn Station in Baltimore, became my own little mobile restoration retreat. Since I didn't have to deal with the stresses of driving and traffic, I took advantage of my commuting time by meditating, reading books, and papers and simply reflecting on what was and what could be.

Yep, I was content. I started thinking creatively again. I decided to drink from the spring in Natalie Babbitt's *Tuck Everlasting* and live forever. I envisioned myself back on top again. I soon began to long for a place to retreat from all the external noise and distractions. I needed a place where I could get focused and remain focused. That's when I discovered this healing place in the Mother Mary Lange room at St. Francis Catholic School in Baltimore.

At the end of my workday, I would often go to that for prayer. It was in this room that I learned that St. Frances was founded in 1828 as an independent Roman Catholic school, and it is the first and oldest Black Catholic school in the United States. Mother Mary Lange was the first ever African American Mother Superior. She founded the Oblate Sisters of Providence. As I took in all this newfound history, I was reminded of my trips to Philadelphia while I was in college to visit the first A.M.E church and learn of Richard Allen and Absalom Jones. *It is so empowering when we center ourselves on the strong history of our people.* I reveled in the cultural pride of our ancestors. With a prayer came my plan. This was when I began to see things turning around for me.

I developed such great friendships with gentle people who cared that I began to open up. There was one person who honored me with a safe space to release and begin my restoration journey. Linda Wilson was the school's guidance counselor and my Wonder Woman. I called her that because she resembled the actress Linda Carter as a young woman. She was loved by every student. Eventually, I ended up sitting on the sofa in her office and confiding in her. She let me know in a nonjudgmental way that she had sensed that things were a total mess for me. She listened and simply became that sounding board that I so appreciated. I was a very private person (clearly, not anymore), but Linda had a way about her that let me know I was safe with her.

I truly believe that God placed me at this Catholic school to be in touch with my past upbringing. It was the perfect environment for my healing process to begin. I had been hired to teach the social justice course as part of their Religion curriculum. The leadership took a risk with me, but they believed that I was the right person for the job. And the job was perfect for me. I had seven classes filled with pure joy, connection, and love. There were courses entitled social justice/teaching social change. Any Catholic school teacher is familiar with this curriculum. I had a dynamic class of seniors, including Lamar Prillman, who not only soaked up every developmental theory; he was the epitome of Black Excellence. Most of the kids would tell me how much they learned from me. Little did they know that they were my lifeline and my connection to my past private schooling. We spent most of our days in that beautiful Mother Mary Lange Room, where we studied the book of Mark in the New Testament. I used to distribute Daily Bread sheets quite similar to the Social Justice teacher's "Woof" sheets from high school. I'll tell you a little about Robert Hoderny in a few. In these classes, we had a direct link to a bible verse daily as we tackled some tough social justice issues. It was the most transforming experience as we prayed daily, five to seven times a day. I truly felt that I was where I was meant to be. I wasn't aware then, but some years later, not only was my bankruptcy removed, but I had a new home, a credit score of 750, and managed to pay off my student loans.

As a single parent, I need to give myself more credit. I had to get back on my feet again and taking a pay cut from teaching in the Public School system placed me directly into a lower income for me to apply for a DC housing program. Who said that this single mother wouldn't get back on top? I developed a plan and didn't allow anything or anyone to stop me. I received some assistance to buy the home through the program and eventually sold it. Shortly after, there was no need for the program as I was able to buy my 3rd house and still put money away to save in 2018. Isn't that what most of the folks in these 2 income homes do? As a DC native, I strongly felt that I deserved a piece of DC just like anyone else. No one was going to push me out of DC, where I was born and raised. Hmm, although these DC taxes may push me out though, that's for sure. My time in Baltimore was short-lived but served a purpose. The disadvantage was having to leave my private school environment, but I kept St. Frances in my heart. I walked directly in God's unconditional love, and the memory of the traumatic experiences started to fade with forgiveness every day. When we feel good about ourselves, we make others feel good. Mother Mary Lange, Pray for us!

Robert Hoderny

First of all, I had amazingly inspirational teachers who influenced me at a young age. I've already told you about my time at Carroll. Well, I mentioned Robert Hoderny a few chapters back. He was my 11th-grade social justice teacher. I'm certain that almost all Carroll alum who encountered our Mr. Robert Hoderny would agree that he not only taught the requisite content but he opened our young hearts. Many of us who dared to venture into his classroom has incorporated his perspective into our teaching philosophies and carried on his legacy. He touched so many lives with his enthusiasm and love for the oppressed and marginalized people in society. He introduced me to the teaching and beliefs of Mother Teresa, Dorothy Day, Mitch Snyder, Gandhi, and a host of others, alongside the traditional heroes we learned about in African American studies.

I frequently leaned on those memories while working at St. Frances and sharing stories of Mr. Hoderny with my students. As part of the program at St. Frances, students volunteered to serve the homeless in a local soup kitchen. It was similar to the community service hours we earned at Carroll while serving at Zacchaeus Soup Kitchen in downtown NW DC.

I vividly recall that day I was serving in the soup kitchen, and I looked up and stared right into the face of a woman who had lived across the street from our old apartment. A fleeting glimmer of recognition crossed her face as our eyes made contact, and before I could say a word, she fled the soup kitchen line. She'd had five children, and my mom used to give her some of my old clothes. I remember feeling so bad when their family was evicted, and her children were placed into the foster care system. On that day, I promised my 17-year-old self that I would always remember that no matter what struggles I had in life, someone else had it worse. Words couldn't describe my sadness as I watched her disappear from my sight. I would have liked to have reconnected and shown her that I cared.

When I became a teacher, I re-created some of the same experiences I had in high school. One of those experiences involved going to see the musical Les Misérables. This truly sparked my love of theatre and plays during my college days.

It was 2001; I was teaching at WMST and dating my then fiancé. My 11th graders had just completed a unit on The Scarlet Letter. I won't go into detail about how fun a Reader's theatre can get once Hester, the main character, becomes the single parent branded with an "S." I had the belief that if everyone learned the plot and all literary elements that we could spice it up a little bit. Shortly after, we read excerpts from Hugo's Les Misérables. I wanted to recreate the same experience Hoderny had created for us in high school. I introduced the students to the storyline; the CD, and we studied and sang the soundtrack for several months until they knew every line. My next step was to get funded for the trip to Broadway. As I marched into the principal's office, he greeted me knowingly, "Roxborough, what is it that you need now?" Mr. James D. Ricks had become accustomed to my almost weekly visits to his office, so he already knew that I wanted money for something for our students. I was always met with his stern demeanor, but I didn't care. I had my way of charming and persuading him to get what I wanted every single time. I called the Box Office for ticket sales in New York and talked them into selling us discounted tickets for our "At Risk" youth. An entire 11th-grade class enjoyed a day trip to New York City with their parents having to pay little to nothing. We left at 6:30am and arrived in NYC by 10:30am. We ate lunch and shopped a while before we made our way to the theater to see the 3-hour musical.

Our troupe of 75 plus flowed out of the theatre, hurrying our way to the bus to head back to DC. As we made our way, a kid and a chaperone shouted out in concert, "That's Michael Jackson!" Our group started to whooping and hollering as Michael waved from the balcony above. The energy was palpable as we hopped onto the bus and made our way back to DC. Everyone was home by 11pm or so.

14

Twin's Mentors

On any given day, you can best believe that I am socializing with somebody somewhere. The professional relationships I developed at WMST, Anacostia, and Saint Frances were solid as a rock. I met Tina Fletcher while I was working as a Dean at Anacostia, along with the dynamic Coco Benitez, who is now a wonderful health and wellness Coach. I have always admired Coco's spirit and energy. Like Tina, she was always giving her time to others unselfishly. Coco and I ran the 9th-grade Academies at Anacostia during the Friendship Charter and Anacostia partnership in 2011. She was incredible to work with; if you recall, my personal life was almost in shambles then. When I showed up to work at 7:30 a.m., I'd open an Academy, and it helped me feel that my life was necessary and I mattered. We were some strong Black women, and together, we rocked.

At the time, Tina was a history teacher at Anacostia, and she and I had tons of conversations about my twins. One day she introduced me to her identical twin sister, Trina Fletcher. I had a knack for attracting twins into my life, and identical twins at that. Soon after, I introduced the Fletcher twins to my girls, and it was love at first sight for all.

My girls attended different schools; most people would say that was really not a logical decision. In hindsight, I would agree because I struggled every morning trying to get them to school on time, one to St. Ann's Academy and the other to St. Augustine. But I had this recurring thought in my head, "Just because I'm a single mom doesn't mean I need to limit myself."

The opportunity had presented itself for the girls to be in separate schools, and I reasoned that they were ALWAYS together. Separate schools meant that they would be called by their own names respectively and be individuals, not just be known as "twins" or "the twins." Each of the girls would have teachers and friends who knew them for their individual personalities, gifts, and talents. It would give my girls the freedom to develop as their unique selves not just as one half of the duo in which they entered the world.

I was a full-time teacher and working towards something—who knows what else I was really into during that year—it's somewhat of a blur. Anyhow, I don't know what I would have done without the Fletcher twins stepping up to love my twins. Trina started picking up my girls in the afternoons. It gave me respite, and I felt I was exposing them to new experiences in the same way that my friends in two-parent households had the opportunity to do for their children. In 2010, the Fletchers launched a mentoring organization called Dreamgirls in DC and Arkansas. My girls were right in the mix, even though they were too young to participate at the time. They would later join when they were older. The program was created to empower and equip young women and girls with the tools to develop positive ambition and focus on pursuing their dreams.

I was so fortunate that the Fletcher twins fell in love with my twins; they practically took them everywhere. Having been raised by a single mom themselves the Fletchers understood my struggles and stepped up to become part of my village. When they left DC and moved back to Arkansas, my heart was entirely broken because every single mom depends on her support system.

Of course, a healthy two-parent household is ideal but I'll continue to point out how fantastic Black children excel despite statistics, research and biases. Criteria for success can be subjective. Single parents deserve more recognition and respect as opposed to stigma.

In 2018, the college enrollment rate was higher for 18- to 24-year-olds who were Asian (59 percent) than for 18- to 24-year-olds who were White (42 percent), Black (37 percent), and Hispanic (36 percent). The overall college enrollment rate has increased since 2000. (Source)

Single mothers have low rates of college degree attainment: as of 2015, just 31 percent of single mothers ages 25 and older held a bachelor's degree or higher, compared with 54 percent of comparable married mothers and 40 percent of comparable women overall (IWPR 2017e). (Source)

The overall graduation rate was 56% of those who attended, but in only two groups was the rate over half: for students with married birth parents and those living with divorced mothers. The graduation rate was under half for all the other family types, with the lowest rates for students raised by grandparents and foster parents. (Source + Photo Below)

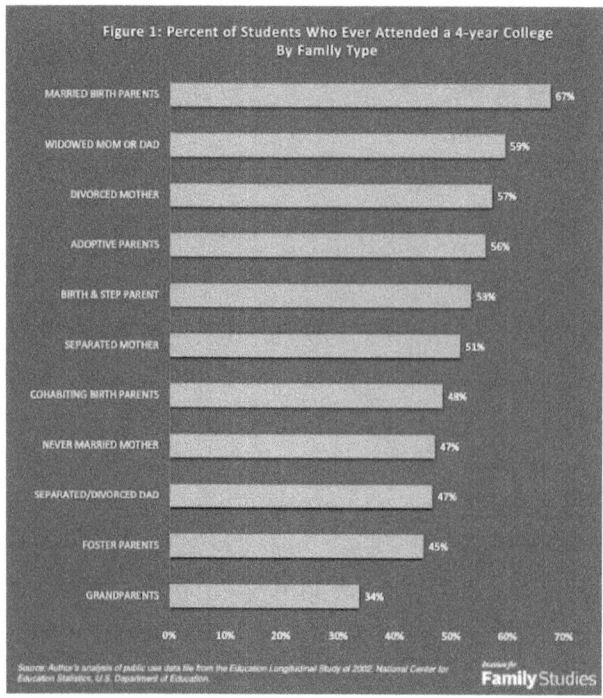

15

Lionel

"May I speak to Ms. Roxborough, please…" Intimacy resonated from every syllable each time I heard those words dripping from his lips and electrifying the phone and my body all at the same time. Just thinking about it still sends a little shiver down my back. What?! My marriage may have died…but I didn't!

A Lion found his way into my life in 2009 through a mutual friend on Facebook. He became my respite, my romantic escape whenever I needed shelter from the turbulent reality of my life. We connected on so many levels almost instantaneously. We talked intensely for three weeks sharing stories of how we'd both grown up in DC. He had also grown up without his father, and I hung on his every word. I confided in him. I shared my fears and insecurities and my joyful thoughts. In every single thing I shared, he supported me emotionally, and it made me feel so special and so cared for.

I found myself becoming addicted to his attentiveness, and it elevated me from the angry morbid place I had been stuck in mentally and emotionally. My heart cried out with joy; it felt so damn good to feel wanted again.Every time we were together, I remember thinking, *why couldn't our paths have crossed earlier*. He was filling in the void and blank spots in my life. As he and I spent more time together, I began thinking about ol' Dude less and less.

At 6'8", Lionel was my gentle giant. He was bald with an athletic build. He was fine! I'll never forget our first kiss. We had met at the Starbucks on Georgia Avenue. It was cloudy and rainy, but it didn't bother us in the least. We had talked for hours. As we stood outside of the store, I kissed him and oooh oooh chile'! Every nerve in my body came to life again. I hadn't felt anything close to what I felt that day in years. I believe that I fell in lust again...I do say lust ah...cause that's exactly what it was. Shit, after the marriage I had...hey, why not?

I still recall how we had gazed into each other's eyes as he held and cuddled me after we became intimate for the first time. He had no clue that it was the first time in years that I had felt so completely open and close to a man. As my hands caressed the scar on his body, left from a surgery he had in high school, I wondered, *where had he been all my life?*

Those moments with him shielded me from the devastation of knowing and meditating on the fact that my husband was not who I thought he was or who I wanted him to be. This Lion was just what I needed, at that time in my life, and a part of me felt that he needed to be there just as much as I needed him to be.

In those moments, Lionel completely filled every void for me. He was the dad I never had, the uncle, the aunt, or even the cousin that should have been there for me. He made me feel safe.

He was so nurturing. His daily calls at 6:30 a.m. strengthened me each morning. He took care of me emotionally— and physically. It was that intimacy that made me feel attractive and worthy again. It was honestly not love I had been seeking, but validation. This was just the feeling Lionel gave me.

My cravings for validation quickly fed into a mental habit of overindulgence in sex with Lionel. I was numb to the thought of love at that point. I just wanted to feel good. I stole away whenever I had an opportunity to be with my Lionel. I should have had my ass in therapy instead of quickies and not-so-quickies on the weekends and weekdays at his place, hotels, his truck, and a football field. Now don't get me wrong, I needed to be held emotionally, but perhaps, just maybe…this Lion was there for me to simply get it in. That's really what it was. I am not gonna lie; sometimes that's exactly what a gal needs, ya know!

I mean, think about it. This sexist society teaches women that in order for us to feel completely whole, we have to be tied into a relationship with a man. Mind you, these relationships can be very toxic or even co-dependent. I was in-tuned with my sexuality, and it didn't have a damn thing to do with needing a relationship. Hell, sometimes women can utilize men for our sexual needs too. We have been taught to suppress our sexuality which is the polar opposite of the oversexualized images we see of Black women in the media today.

I'm here to tell you that a woman with class can have a discrete intimate relationship without the world knowing. It is possible to carry yourself as an upstanding dignified woman and still "get yours" at the same time. It's not about being tied down all the time. Some women are independent and career-oriented, but they still want the benefits of having the goodies that a relationship has to offer in a carefree, uncommitted connection.

If that is the case, it's important to establish boundaries in which the involved parties understand that what they share is in the now. It was the carefree, fun times spent with my Lion that helped me get through that last act of betrayal of my husband remarrying days after our divorce was final.

Lionel listened to me and consoled me. It was Lionel's listening ear and that cute, funny ass chuckle that made me smile and remember the poem I had written years ago during my senior year about a lover. I tweaked it and made it relevant to him, my rebound lover. I felt it was so fitting to describe our romance.

I do believe, in hindsight, that I definitely should not have jumped into a sexual relationship; however, hell…if people can smoke weed (no judgments, LOL) and drink almost every damn day to escape their reality in life, then I can have an illicit yet fulfilling love affair.

As I look back, I know that we really didn't have much in common with one another, but it was what it was. Isn't that what we tell ourselves when we know we could very well make better choices? *It is what it is.*

Whatever the case, he helped heal many of the wounds ripped open from my not knowing my worth and being married to someone who wasn't worthy of my love. Hell, those stolen moments allowed me to pretend that my life really wasn't falling apart. That little piece of my life was carved just for him, MAY EYES.

In my eyes, I've planted you windowsill carnations that —I breathed in from the sun to bear you fruit trees-your ruffled yellow charm made me smile gillyflowers on the mornings at 7am, or in the afternoons a little after 4:30 when you spoke with me- Away that day in August has taken our root bearing stems —Love, I only hope our bulbs will bloom again-From the seeds, we were rooted, seems like the other day-cultivated Dianthus flowers inside of me-I see Brown sugar touches from the windowsill coffee pot and forgotten April droplets of water pillows-No more brittle Billie Holiday weeping willows-Love when our favorite month of May rolls around. Summer is fusion for our little carnations- I want us to walk gracefully, as branching stems from the drained, soil-continuing to love perfectly in purple, yellow, and pink, tall voices that speak many buds of sun dreams.

16

Fresh Start...

In August 2018, a new me emerged with excellent credit and a desire for something new. I made up my mind to leave the DC Public School system. It had been almost five years since I'd worked with teenagers; oh, how I'd missed it so much. To be honest, even more than that, I was just jaded and frustrated by the system and all its bureaucracy. My mind began to stir with thoughts of creating something of my own.

One day my mom came to me seemingly out of the blue, "Erin, I want to work with babies again; why not open your own childcare, and I will work with your infants?"

That was easier said than done, but once I made up my mind to do it, I contacted OSSE, and what was designed for up to 90 days to complete, I did it in 30 days! I really believe it was my anxiety and fear of failure that caused me to push myself to take all the food certifications and all the other requirements from the DCRA in record time. There was this annoying and patronizing little voice that kept at me, *Who the hell do you think you are to leave a career?* But I stayed focused on my goal. I mean, I had years of experience established history of positive and wonderful relationships with students and their families; who was I not to do it?

I intentionally created a space in my home where my new classroom could accommodate lots of positive interactions with each child throughout the day. I quickly joined national organizations such as the NAEYC, the local DCAEYC, and the DC Child Care Association. If I was gonna do it, I had to do it the right way.

I needed to remain connected to children and to people who love children. Most importantly, I reconnected to my purpose with a new energy and focus that I had been missing for some time. I was creating an environment where children could feel loved and safe. This new Erin was still rooted in the Erin from long ago, who always took care of other people's children; she just had a new platform. This entire home daycare thing was just the perfect idea. I could still advocate for children much like I did as a teacher. Yep, once I became licensed, I became an advocate for quality family childcare and delved into research-based curriculums aligned with Head Start, like ABC Mouse or Hooked on Phonics.

I continue working and walking in my purpose, which is dedicated to providing children with the tools they need to face the world, especially since I finally learned some of the tools needed to sustain me!

After everything I had overcome, I developed some more backbone, charisma, and hope, along with this relentless optimistic attitude that change is actually good and possible.

During the pandemic, I am proud to say that I picked up all kinds of new self-care routines because, for most Black women who were raised in homes with strong, responsible women, we must take breaks from ALL of our responsibilities.

Our purpose becomes larger than ourselves when we recognize and acknowledge the value of the contributions we make to our community. Self-care must be a priority. I learned that the hard way. I promised myself that I would attach myself to three or more self-care routines each week, walking, Zumba, yoga, and practicing mindfulness and communing with nature just like I did during my teen years. I walked around DC with Emerson's Self Reliance or any Henry David Thoreau book held tightly in my hand. I have Jim Mumford and Elizabeth Purcell to thank for that.

Hell, dealing with depression and anxiety, you've got to be intentional. First to heal personally from the dramas and traumas in your history, then the next step should include reflecting on the impact in your professional life. One thing I will admit is that I still want to work with teenagers or young adults. As I told you, in 2005, I started to work towards my second Masters in School Counseling. I had a vision: Erin Roxborough, MA, LPC, is a Licensed Professional Counselor with 10 years of clinical experience, 15 years of teaching experience, and 1 year as a parent of identical twin daughters. LOL. As you can clearly see, things didn't quite work out that way. I was on track to reach my prize, and then—you know the story; after the divorce, I had to balance single motherhood of twins and full-time work, which didn't leave time for much else. Although I was close to completing the program, I couldn't commit to all the extra hours required for the remaining coursework and practicum. So, I switched the plan and received an individualized master's in human development. You know, there are times I still wish I could have my private practice to serve children, teens, and families.

Now that you know most of my personal business, we should make it OUR business to push for mandatory mental health awareness in schools where kids can get credit for it.

Let's talk about depression, anxiety, eating disorders, racial issues, and mental disorders more openly and often. Most importantly, we can all benefit from developing better coping skills. Let's not have any more arguments with folks about whether or not racism exists. I used to make copies of excerpts from Derrick Bell's Faces at the Bottom of the Well; grab an address for that birthday card and mail it!!! Sheesh! Will someone remind me again why we are still debating whether racism exists? But we also have to remember that so does unconditional love, isn't that the lesson we're supposed to be learning? So, we should go ahead and start there, or pick up and continue whatever we have to do to maintain wonderful, positive, and life-sustaining relationships with each other. Well, thank you so much for sticking around with me and listening to my story. Sharing is caring, as they say. You can always email me and tell me how much I bored you.

Dear Father,

Allow me to introduce myself. I am Erin Roxborough, divorced, mother of two amazing young women, extraordinary educator, business owner, mentor, and your one and only daughter and I have Daddy issues. As I sit and write this letter, I acknowledge that you might never read it. Hmph, actually, I know you will never read it. How do I know? Because I do not exist to you.

The truth is, it really doesn't matter whether you read this or not because I'm writing it for me. You see, when I was young, writing became my outlet and release for all the things I couldn't say out loud. What's interesting is that it was always easy for me to speak up and speak out loudly for other people who were disrespected, mistreated, taken advantage of, or harmed in some way. I just could never do it for myself. Oh, I wanted to, but something always seemed to stop me. Perhaps it was the persistent nagging thoughts of feeling unworthy, less-than, out of place, weird and unwanted by one of the one men who was supposed to love me no matter what. It has taken me decades to find my voice and speak up for myself. I have decided that I will no longer be silent.

They say that women "marry" their fathers. I can testify to that theory. Despite my every intention to marry someone who loved me unconditionally and supported my dreams and aspirations, I ended up with a man who, although he was there (at times) physically, was absent emotionally and in all the other ways that really count. In hindsight, I can see the red flags that I ignored and dismissed. At that point in my life, I had no way of knowing how my relationship with you, or lack thereof, was clouding my perception of what a healthy relationship between a man and a woman looked like.

Mom poured into me all that she possibly could to build me up and show me the woman I could be. I never once doubted or questioned her love for me. I've felt it all the days of my life. I needed her, and I needed you too. With all she was and still is to me, she is not my father.

You don't know this because we never spoke of such things, but all I ever wanted from you as I was growing up was to be Daddy's Little Girl. I wanted to sit on your knee as you told me made-up adventure stories and shared Eskimo kisses and ice cream cones, to be tickled until I couldn't catch my breath, and to stand on your feet as you swirled me around and around at the Father Daughter Dance. Believe it or not, I wanted to experience the embarrassment and wonder of watching you interrogate any boy who dared to ask me on a date…but …it was all simply a wish and a hope that I had to lay to rest a long time ago.

You see, our Daddy-Daughter history is littered with countless acts and endless years of your refusing to see me, treating me as an inconvenience, and denying my existence. Even at nine years old, I felt it. I was an undesirable and inconvenient obligation, but as a dutiful Roxborough man, you would never shirk your duty. Sometimes I wish you had. It would have saved me years of wondering why you never hugged and kissed me or showed even a modicum of interest in my schooling, my likes or dislikes. Yet I persisted.

Maybe it was never your intention, but I always felt as if I was asking for too much to have a relationship with you. When I was in college, I would sit on the sidelines of conversations about what my girlfriends would never confess to their fathers. It wasn't an issue for me; I never did anything that required a confession, but more importantly, I knew you would never ask. We have had brief conversations over the years, and at times I'd try to share how proud I was of this accomplishment or that one. When I received my second master's degree in education, I was excited to share it with you and the rest of the family. I was so proud! You asked, "Was that all I could think of to be?" Somehow, I'd hoped that that conversation would end differently. Maybe a word or two from you affirming my accomplishment or a simple "Good job," but as it happened many times before I walked away from the discussion under the shadow of your disapproval. I don't recall you ever saying that you were proud of me. What I do remember…and will never forget is the day you told me to never call you or contact you ever again. The remains of my broken hope of ever having a relationship with you were shattered!

But as your dutiful daughter, I have honored and obeyed your request. Each year, the opportunity to celebrate birthdays, recitals, and holidays with your daughter and granddaughters rolls by without any sign from you that you desire to get to know us. It saddens me. I can't fathom my life at any point without my girls being at the center. The joy of watching them take their first steps, learn to ride bikes, and discover the world around them…how could anyone choose to deny themselves that blessing from above.

I've tried to rationalize the why; maybe it was the fact that I was the first girl in the family, and since you didn't have any sisters, you just didn't know what to do with me. Or maybe it was the proverbial "baby mama drama," but we both know that wasn't it. You and Mom have always had a respectful relationship. I've resigned myself to the fact that I will never know why you didn't carve out a small space for me in your life.

Whatever your reason, I've come to a place in my life where I know who I am, even without your acknowledgement of my lineage. I was and still am your biological daughter, but that's not all I am.

You see, I know who I am and whose I am. I thank God every day for a mother who made sure that I had a relationship with my Heavenly Father. He has kept me and sustained me more than you'll ever know.

As a grown woman, I have forgiven you to heal myself. I have reconciled that you will never be the father you should have been to me. But that little girl is still hurt. If I'm honest with myself, it still hurts to know that I wasn't enough, that you never saw any value in me. That you couldn't love me for me because I am your child.

Daddy, the brokenhearted little girl in me, still hopes that one day my phone will ring, and on the other end, she'll hear you say, "Hey baby girl, how's your day going?" While I let her continue to hope, I will carry on living the life that I have chosen, to raise strong women who know that they are loved and valued simply for being who they are, to teach, coach, and mentor other people's children because they have value too and to forgive those who have hurt me. I will pray that one day you will understand that a daughter is a father's gift from God. But until that time comes, I will continue to love you from afar and pray for your broken heart every day.

I love you, Daddy,

Erin

Memory Lane

*Pic of my mom when I was 10 years old, her name is
Jacquelyn Brannon.*

Pic of me with my twin daughters, Alanna
(to the left to the eye if looking at the photo)
and Arianna...8 years old.

Pic of my twins with their twin mentors, Tina Fletcher to the left of the eye looking at the photo, she's directly above my twin daughter, Arianna (other twin sister) she's to the right of the eye looking the the photo directly above my twin daughter, Alanna.

*Pic of me returning back to Syracuse University to visit. The big flex for me
was that I just paid off all of my student loans despite my
failed marriage, foreclosure, etc.*

Pic of me with one of college friends, Qiana Williams.

My dear mother.

Me with one of co-worker/friends, Linda Wilson along with other past coworker, Angela -Thorpe Johnson at St. Frances.

Me with college friend, Keisha Campbell,

This pic is also a huge deal to me I was age 35, in 2009 in green dress... I felt so Tomboyish, but had just gotten my Panther tattoo and from the advice from a close sister friend who told me to try not to "look like what i was going through" during that same year of 2009... year of loss of job, bankruptcy, foreclosure, etc.

Me at age 39 in 2013 - This pic was a huge deal for me because I had just gotten my excellent credit back despite the bankruptcy, etc-- and it was my 39th bday and I felt fantastic and blessed.

Resources

Domestic Violence

DC Safe

https://www.Dc safe.org/

My Sister's Place in NW DC

https://www.domesticshelters.org/help/dc/washington/20017/my-sister-s-place

DC Coalition Against Domestic Violence

https://dccadv.org/

Mental Health

1. https://www.namidc.org/

2. https://www.rosscenter.com/

3. https://strengthinourvoices.org/

4. https://www.thenationalcouncil.org/

5. https://www.catholiccharitiesdc.org/acs/

Alcoholism

https://some.org/

The Wells House

https://www.thewhouse.org/

Lasting Change

https://www.samaritaninns.org/samaritan-inns-media/blog/

Samaritan Inn Foundations

https://www.foundationsrecoverycenter.com

About the Author

Erin Roxborough, a proud DC native, resides in the vibrant Deanwood area of Northeast DC. As a devoted mother of identical twin daughters, she is deeply committed to their well-being and education. Erin's journey in academia began at Syracuse University, where she earned a BA in African-American Studies. Driven by her passion for education, she pursued further studies at Syracuse University's School of Education, obtaining a Master's degree in Secondary Education. Seeking a comprehensive understanding of human development, she also completed a Master's degree in Human Development from The George Washington University. With an impressive career spanning over two decades, Erin has contributed her expertise to various educational institutions, including charter, private, and two public school systems. In 2018, fueled by her dedication to nurturing young minds, Erin took a significant step by opening her own licensed childcare center, Ms. Rox's Child Care, LLC. Her unwavering commitment to providing a nurturing environment and quality care for children is a testament to her passion for education and child development.